"*Peggy Flynn has more experience providing care and support to terminally ill people than anybody I know. Her ability to guide those in her care to a passing suffused with peace and dignity is a God-given talent, one that comes from her head, her heart and her spirit. I urge you to read this book; if not, you risk missing a unique opportunity to learn intimate details about caregiving from a true veteran and practitioner of the art.*"

—Jon D. Kaiser, M.D., Physician and Author of *Healing HIV*

◆　　◆　　◆

"*The Caregiving Zone offers a direct, practical and open path to the contact sport of caregiving—both giving and receiving—for readers willing to have honest, rousing and ultimately life affirming conversations about being alive and dying.*"

—Jonathan Berkeley PhD

◆　　◆　　◆

"*When I was asked to apply for a job as a hospice chaplain, I spent much of the interview nervously wondering when they would realize I had no real experience and they had made a mistake. "What would you do if..." asked the social worker. I went blank. Then I thought, "What would Peggy do?" I got the job. After six years of hospice work, I am still in awe of the inspiration and insight knowing Peggy brings to my work and my life. This book will give you a context for living—not just surviving—in the presence of the transition we call death. Its balance of practical, spiritual and emotional stories will guide, encourage and sustain you. The topic of this book is not easy, but it is essential. Thanks to Peggy, I have come to realize that death can be a life-giving opportunity if you know how to prepare for it."*

—The Rev. Kevin Yell

◆　　◆　　◆

"Peggy Flynn is nothing short of brilliant. The Caregiving Zone provides a breathtakingly honest insight into making the most out of the end of life. Most of us live in denial that we and those we love will die, thus providing an excuse not to plan and think. Ms. Flynn takes a baseball bat to the wall of denial and forces us to take an honest look at ourselves and at the choices we make for the future. This book is uplifting and inspirational and provides a guide for us to make the most out of the end of our days."

—Tracy Salkowitz MSW

◆　　◆　　◆

"I was talking with my mother—69 this year—and I had her read the chapter on Independence—one of her areas of concern. We had a great talk about it…[the book] is so easy to read, yet so rich in context."

—Christy Redford

The Caregiving Zone

The Caregiving Zone

Peggy Flynn, M.A.
Executive Director of The Good Death Institute

iUniverse, Inc.
New York Lincoln Shanghai

The Caregiving Zone

iUniverse books may be ordered through booksellers or by contacting:

iUniverse
2021 Pine Lake Road, Suite 100
Lincoln, NE 68512
www.iuniverse.com
1-800-Authors (1-800-288-4677)

ISBN-13: 978-0-595-40649-4 (pbk)
ISBN-13: 978-0-595-85015-0 (ebk)
ISBN-10: 0-595-40649-1 (pbk)
ISBN-10: 0-595-85015-4 (ebk)

Printed in the United States of America

To my grandmother, Katie Curtin Sullivan

A strange thing happens to the man who really loves, for even before his own death his life becomes a life with the dead. Could a true lover ever forget his dead? When one has really loved, his forgetting is only apparent: he only seems to get over his grief. The quiet and composure he gradually retains are not a sign that things are as they were before, but a proof that his grief is ultimate and definitive. It shows that a piece of his own heart has really died and is now with the living dead. This is the real reason he can weep no more.

—Karl Rahner
Encounters with Silence

Contents

Acknowledgements

How do I write acknowledgments that would do justice to all the people, living and dead, who made primary contributions to my apprenticeship and to this book? There are too many to name individually and I dread hurting anyone's feelings. It will have to be enough to say that I am eternally grateful to everyone who has let me be part of their particular journey through the valley of the shadow of death and to everyone who supported me in so many varied ways. This book is your book. To each of you—*you know who you are.* Thank you.

I also want to thank everyone who has contributed to making The Good Death Institute a place for research and education about dying and death. The ideas in the book are a direct result of the discussions that have taken place under its auspices.

I need to give special credit to David Webber who has been my mentor during a twenty-year ongoing conversation about all sorts of journeys through the valleys of the shadow. His searching questions and technical expertise transformed a raw manuscript into a book. Thank you, David.

There is one other person who has been a constant companion through the ups and downs of the start-up years and rewrite after rewrite. Her many contributions helped this book come to be at last. Thank you, AnnD Canavan.

Introduction

"I was not aware of having any special insight into dying, nor did I have any special interest in terminal care. My involvement came, I think, from a basic sense of justice and a sense of pragmatism."

—Ira Byock, MD (Byock 1997, 29)

I have often been asked why I volunteer to work with the terminally ill. I sense when people ask me this question that they are projecting onto me some grand, compassionate heart. The words of Dr. Ira Byock quoted above seem more accurate. I didn't start out to work with the dying. I wanted to be a laying-on-of-hands healer. I wanted to make people well. In 1989 I met up with Dr. Jon Kaiser and was launched into the HIV epidemic in San Francisco, where I saw illness and death in young and beautiful faces. Many people were responding to the crisis, but I was in a unique position because I did massage and bodywork and had hospice experience.

If during a massage session, a client talked about his diagnosis and prognosis, I would ask some basic questions about dying. An especially important question was "What's your worst fear?" When I would hear from a man in his twenties that he feared to die alone, given that he and his family were estranged and that he had buried all his friends, my reaction was usually fury. Something had to be done and it might just have to be me who would do it. It was a matter of justice and pragmatism, not warm fuzzy feelings. The truth is, warm fuzzy feelings are nice but they really don't have enough *juice* to get you through the hard times. When my heart gets weary, broken and confused, I am kept going by justice, pragmatism and a dash of mercy.

Over time I've become more adept at listening for the moment when a person begins to speak about the dawning reality that his or her life will end. These first attempts are halting and clumsy, like an adolescent trying to find words for embarrassing hormonal changes. Often the moment is casually slipped in among other moments. Beginnings are such delicate times.

I am a practicing Catholic raised on *The Lives of the Saints* and images of the compassionate Heart of Jesus. When I was fifteen I read the Boddhisatva vow and was thrilled to the core of my adolescent soul: "For as long as space exists and sentient beings endure, may I too remain to dispel the misery of the world." (Rinpoche 1993, 365) The bulk of my first career focused on computer office applications at several start-ups and large corporations. The work was intellectually challenging and financially rewarding but largely devoid of meaning. I was going crazy trying to reconcile my ideals with working sixty-plus hours a week producing documentation that was obsolete before it was published. I helped out with friends and family who were sick or dying and worked as a caregiver to support myself through school, but it wasn't enough. I had money but no meaning.

As my forties loomed I decided to go for meaning. I wanted to work with individuals on issues relating to the second half of life, so I completed a Masters degree at Goddard College, focusing on the psychology and physiology of aging. I also knew that I wanted to integrate my passion for hands-on healing into this work. I wanted to be able to work with people in an in-depth way that addressed both their current physical ills and their underlying patterns of stress. I studied Structural Integration—the technique pioneered by Ida Rolf—with Joseph Heller. In 1989, with a brand-new Masters degree and bodywork credential, I opened an office in San Francisco. I was ready for clients and to make my contribution to the world of gerontology. But life had other plans for me.

Given that most people past the age of fifty have one or more health issues, I went looking for a physician who would provide some supervision and, I hoped, referrals. After many unanswered letters and unreturned phone calls I was referred to Dr. Jon Kaiser, who had started providing complementary therapy to individuals with HIV. He was intrigued by the possibilities of using touch therapy on clients with immune system diseases and we began working together. At that point in the epidemic, fear about any physical contact with someone with HIV was rampant. People worried about transmission through sweat and tears. For me, here was my dream come true—a full practice of clients who had serious medical issues and wanted to work the full body/mind/spirit continuum. I found I could use all of my graduate school training because, no matter their chronological age, once diagnosed with a (then) terminal illness, my clients were in the second half of their lives.

When people ask me what I am, my answers are usually in the form of what I'm not: I am not a doctor, nurse, social worker or chaplain. Over time I came to realize that my primary credential is that I am a well-informed generalist. I get to see the whole picture, unlike many professionals who operate only within the bounds of their specialty. At various times I am a translator, appointment maker, coordinator, team builder, fundraiser, alarm bell, companion, or guardian. When asked, "Who is my neighbor?" Jesus responded with a parable of a man in crisis and the reaction of three people to his plight, offering us an example of a first responder—The Good Samaritan, also a generalist. So this is what I try to be—a skilled and committed neighbor.

Along the way I realized that I wanted to apply what I had learned over the years on a wider basis. I started The Good Death Institute in 1998 to do research and education about dying and death and the ways these realities play out in the lives of individuals and communities. So far we have produced one research study, *Death and Dying in San Francisco*, and a seven part course *Planning a Good Death: Getting Your House in Order*. In addition we provide information and referrals to individuals, whatever their role, who find themselves in The Caregiving Zone.

In these chapters I wish to share some of what I have learned over the past twenty-five years caring for individuals during their struggles with illness, aging, dying and death. The chapters may be read straight through or in any order you choose. It is not my aim here to present a linear argument leading to a certain conclusion regarding caregiving and its difficulties, of which there are many. I've had more than my share of hair-raising caregiving experiences. Nor do I propose that there is a magic-bullet single solution to address the foreseeable problems of dealing with an aging population, working families, managed healthcare, and possible pandemics.

But I do think that there are reasons to be hopeful. I have witnessed people coming together in marvelous ways to care for their loved ones. I have seen people transformed by their illnesses and dying processes. And I've seen caregivers also transformed by their experiences. Feelings of being trapped in a caregiving situation can be replaced by feelings of accomplishment, tenderness, reconciliation and love. Illness and dying are hard on all concerned, but they need not be hideous. Pain and suffering can be ameliorated. Authentic communication can take place. Old wounds can be healed. A sense of community can be instilled.

The possibilities are truly exciting. Why then is death more often hideous than hard? What prevents individuals and families from distilling meaning and healing from inevitable events? What have people done in the past? Most Americans can trace their roots back to societies that had well-defined belief systems and customs relating to illness, dying and death. For the most part these traditions have not translated well to 21st century urban life and are no longer observed. Unable to rely upon lost traditions, many people find themselves overwhelmed by the imperatives of modern medical technologies that seem to eclipse any other needs and concerns.

What can we do about this void? How is this an opportunity? How can we develop new customs and traditions? How can a family or community of friends take charge of the inevitable facts of illness and death? Is physician-assisted suicide the alternative? How can we as individuals and groups evaluate needs and acquire skills to address these needs based on accumulated experiences both good and bad? In the chapter *Taking Charge of the Inevitable,* I propose a program that makes use of a team of specialists representing the entire spectrum of contemporary concerns about illness and dying. The team would provide assessments and ongoing coaching to individuals and families in The Caregiving Zone. I have included at the end of the book a bibliography of authors whose ideas are central to my work and a list of Internet resources to which I refer most often.

I hope that my ideas and stories will help promote conversations about vital issues that arise for all those involved in the caregiving process. Honest and open conversations are one antidote to the preventable pain caused by ignorance and fear. One of the major obstacles to a good death, however you may envision it, is the taboo against talking about it. This taboo prevents conversation, especially early on in the process when open discussion is crucial. It is essential to ask questions, obtain vital information, create intimacy and clarify values. The earlier the better.

I have been privileged to work with hundreds of ill and dying people from initial diagnosis to the moment of death, a process that in some cases lasted more than ten years. We would talk in physician and hospital waiting rooms, at drugstore pick-up windows, in emergency rooms, coffee shops, diners, living rooms, bedrooms. Hours and hours of talking about everything from gossip to blood counts, travel arrangements to life after death. This is their book as much as it is mine.

The Caregiving Zone

"There are only four kinds of people in the world: People, who have been caregivers, people who are currently caregivers, people who will be caregivers, and people who need a caregiver."

—Rosalynn Carter

Imagine that you've gone to the doctor and gotten a diagnosis. You've developed a treatment strategy. Maybe you went by yourself to the drugstore to fill the prescriptions. You come home with one or more orange bottles and printouts detailing side effects. If the problem is an infection, one cycle of antibiotics should take care of it. But what if it is a chronic or potentially terminal condition? Many people choose to manage their own medications to maintain control and privacy. But many will hand the small orange bottles to someone else. That someone else has now entered The Caregiving Zone.

The actors in The Caregiving Zone form a kind of matrix around the person requiring care. The patient is connected to all the others in the caregiving network and they in turn may find themselves connected to each other in various relationships as the illness takes its course. The person's illness affects everyone woven into this matrix. Some may experience the illness as a major blow while others may consider it a minor irritation. The entire relationship matrix is now in The Caregiving Zone. Some people may remain on the periphery, but all are affected. Sometimes an acquaintance becomes a central member of the team. Sometimes a family member needs to move to the periphery because of other responsibilities. Sometimes a complete stranger becomes an integral factor.

When I read books about caregiving, I try to ascertain the author's location in The Zone. An author describes his or her reality from a certain perspective. We need to be aware of our own perspective as well as the perspective of everyone else involved. Experiencing a sickroom is one thing to a once-a-week visitor and quite another to a person living in the house and taking constant care of a dying person. Ground Zero is experienced in one way by a hospice team that comes for brief visits during the last few days or weeks and in another way entirely by a partner or daughter who's been carrying the daily responsibilities for several years. People on the periphery often enter full of enthusiasm, with lists of suggestions and judgments, while the primary caregiver might not be able to remember his or her last full night of sleep.

I distinguish between caregivers and service providers. Service providers, with a few exceptions such as home health aides and visiting nurses, work at facilities like medical offices, law firms or hospitals. They may do home visits, but their primary place of work is a professional setting. They charge for their services and usually refuse service if an individual doesn't have the means to pay. They are available at scheduled times. Their primary allegiance is to their employer. They chose their profession and have committed a great amount of time and energy to the credentialing process. They work within a set structure. Many of them are committed and compassionate people who provide the best possible service, often in spite of the system.

Caregivers, on the other hand, perform most of their services in peoples' homes, assisting with daily activities such as cooking, cleaning, transportation and assisting with medications. Usually the caregiver is not in a position to leave for any length of time. Their schedule is often determined by others, usually service providers, and by the demands of the illness. Emergencies and acute episodes do not make appointments in advance. Caregivers are usually untrained and sometimes drafted by circumstances beyond their control.

One of my pet peeves is when a person declares himself or herself to be, or is described as, living independently, when in fact several of his or her daily activities require regular assistance from family members and friends. I think it would be more honest to say, "I live on my own with regular free help from people who care about me." Saying it this way acknowledges the need for assistance in maintaining autonomy while acknowledging other people's contributions of time and energy.

You encounter the word caregiver more and more often these days. September 15th is even *National Caregiver Day*. Various reports list statistics about caregivers and caregiving. News stories profile individual caregivers. But caregivers are a mostly invisible sector of society and their contributions go largely unnoticed and unpaid.

It is important to realize that many of us will at some time be caregivers and very likely need caregiving ourselves, perhaps simultaneously. I see it with my elderly clients and will probably see more of it as baby boomers continue to age. Many of us will probably not be able to pay for all the care we will require. We will need each other to make a life worth living.

Much has been written about the deep denial of aging, sickness and death in our culture. The advertising industry makes a fortune from our fear and loathing of these realities. We are inundated with images of young, healthy gods and goddesses and the products that supposedly got them to that state. Can you imagine an ad showing someone in a wheelchair selling margarine or someone who is blind demonstrating a new shampoo? Don't disabled people cook and eat or have wonderful hair? Many times I have heard caregivers say that their experiences weren't "like it happens in the movies." I always ask, "Which movie?"

In the Zone

I think of hospitals and medical offices in terms of zones. The emergency room is a zone. The intensive care unit is another zone, as is radiology, nuclear medicine and surgery. Each of these zones is peopled by two distinct entities: specially trained professionals using equipment and procedures designed to address a particular set of physical problems and the individuals whose bodies are the site of the problem.

The Caregiving Zone is doctors' waiting rooms with magazines, uncomfortable chairs and impatient patients; hospital waiting rooms with more magazines, uncomfortable chairs and possibly uncommunicative and unhelpful staff; drug store prescription windows where the clerk rings up hundreds of transactions a day but seldom makes eye contact; and the home where drugs are taken and side-effects experienced and where, eventually, the *Zone* can shrink from the whole house to just the bed and bath. The home can become a temporary infirmary, a mini-nursing home, or a hospice.

Caregiving happens in enclosed spaces, usually way too hot for anyone not in the throes of illness, and crowded with medical staff and equipment. Places that smell of illness and cleaning fluids. Places of fear and claustrophobia. I have spent many days and nights in sickrooms. I have all sorts of ways of dealing with the boredom, the claustrophobia, the smells and the sense of being trapped physically and emotionally. Sometimes they work, sometimes not. Some of these involve tangibles like having projects to do while waiting and rewarding myself with something that brings me pleasure. Some involve intangibles like getting over myself and becoming more compassionate.

My tangible necessities for protracted stays in the Caregiving Zone usually include food, my laptop computer, my knitting and crossword puzzles, my checkbook to balance, serious and not-so-serious reading material, and personal care items like a toothbrush. Because sitting with someone who is sick and maybe dying often brings to mind my own loved ones, I usually have cards, postage stamps and my address book with me. And I have a prayer book and rosary. These are all items that comfort me and restore my equilibrium. If I'm less stressed, it helps the other person relax. I might use these materials or I might not. What is important is that whatever I'm doing be interruptible and non-intrusive. Often I will reward myself after a prolonged stay in the Caregiving Zone. It may be an hour in a coffee shop sipping a latte, or retail therapy at a used bookstore. If the stay was extremely taxing, I may purchase some expensive wool that I'd been eyeing for some time. These things make me happy. As the intensity of a caregiving situation increases, so does the size of the reward.

I also have an intangible inner voice that reminds me in no uncertain terms that I am not the person in pain, that I will walk away from this situation at some point and sit down to a nice dinner, watch some TV, and pet my cats. The person I'm caring for won't. It is a bracing voice that wakes me up when I am sliding into self-pity. The other intangible that serves me well is my spiritual quest for a compassionate heart, especially in situations where my temper is activated. I try to remember that much of the behavior I'm seeing is rooted in old patterns about which I can do very little. But I can recognize when those patterns are activating mine. Because fear usually brings out the worst in us and is the root of most anger, I do my best to reduce the overall level of fear and to provide a competent and peaceful presence, good information, and a shoulder to cry on. All of these methods and tricks, tangible and intangible, help keep me present and sane while I'm in The Zone.

Zone is a wonderfully rich word. It can signify a place, a time and a state of being. Hospitals and doctors' offices are more than places. Time is altered there. Regular time becomes hospital time, time for meds, time between meds, time for tests, waiting time. In these zones we are not in charge. We are supplicants making our case to the guardian at the gate. We need a prescription, information, referrals or an appointment. We ride our own roller coaster: hyper alert, scared, on hold, tired to the bone, frustrated, reassured, bored.

Zones are prime examples of liminal space and time, the space between the places where we normally live our lives. They occupy a different dimension, a world between worlds. Adolescence is another such state. So is the time of engagement to be married. One is neither a child nor an adult, neither single nor married. The diagnosis of serious illness initiates one into a liminal state. One is on the threshold of a major event: one's own death

Performers, artists and athletes describe being in The Zone. They describe a moment in time when all of the physical training, education and dreams of achievement come together and the body and mind move effortlessly to actualize their vision. Does this apply to caregiving? Do any of us associate terms like "physical training" or "dreams of achievement" with realities like hours of waiting, insults from service providers, supporting a person vomiting into a toilet, coping with finances, or trying to get results from 1-800-try-and-make-us? How does one train for this? Most people find themselves suddenly launched (or is it dropkicked?) into the role of caregiver. They're going along with their lives and word comes that a partner has cancer or a parent has congestive heart failure, and suddenly they find themselves cast in the role of caregiver.

The realities encountered by these new actors in The Caregiving Zone don't resemble much what they've seen on television or at the movies, which constantly bombard us with images of the young and aggressively well. Older people, if depicted at all, might be crotchety but they're able-bodied and funny and economically self-sufficient. They dress fashionably, play sports and delight in each other's company. The main question seems to be when to take the Viagra. We're encouraged to look forward to a time when our children have left home and we too can dress well, play sports and delight in each other's company in well-planned economic self-sufficiency. Reality, of course, is very different. When suddenly faced with cancer, Alzheimer's disease or diabetes, our lifestyle changes significantly. Few people, if any, in this situation are concerned with dressing well or taking Viagra.

Being a caregiver requires assuming a stance in three senses of the word. It is a way of standing or being placed in a position of responsibility for someone vulnerable. It is also an intellectual and emotional attitude, clarifying values and giving one the strength to keep commitments. It is a position of the whole body assumed by an athlete, such as the still place to which martial artists return between moves, both at rest and ready to move in whatever direction the situation requires.

It seems contradictory to be on the one hand dropkicked into a situation and on the other having to make ethical choices. The question is how to transform what can seem like prison into a life challenge. Locating oneself appropriately is crucial to understanding specific stress factors and necessary supports. What exactly is the situation? What are the challenges? What is my role?

My father called me one day in 1990 from the recovery room of a hospital in Chicago after having surgery for colon cancer. I was living in San Francisco at the time providing hospice care for total strangers and already in the thick of the HIV epidemic. He asked me to come home and take care of him, saying the doctors had given him six months to live. I said no. I had made commitments. If he wanted me to take care of him, it had to be in California. That was in mid-summer. Within six months he had relocated to San Francisco. He would live another couple of years.

This was a major ethical challenge for me. He was a difficult man and we had a miserable history. And he was my father. Loyalty is important to me. I also knew that I had the skills, family information, and support system to make his last years less damaging to my siblings and myself. Maybe some healing might happen in the process. Given our history, I wasn't looking for a made-for-television happy ending. I just hoped for intergenerational damage control.

It was obvious when he arrived that he was not dying. I remembered that his mother was still alive and in her nineties. He was only in his early seventies. I was immediately depressed. I had to reach into myself and out into my world for strength. He was as ornery and duplicitous as ever. I should have verified that terminal diagnosis. But now, here he was in my life again. I set four conditions for how things were going to work based on my need to conserve my energy and safety.

First, given the need to keep a close eye on his care, I got him an apartment in my building. This conserved my energy. Second, since there was a huge difference between how he treated me in public versus in private, I seldom went to his apartment. We met regularly at the coffee shop near the building. We also went to church together most Sundays. Third, he agreed that I would meet all his doctors and be his medical power of attorney. I went with him to every important appointment and got the facts. Fourth, he managed his own diabetic care and I arranged for someone to clean and do his laundry.

I saw my role as manager of his situation. My job was to ensure his safety. I was his daughter, not his nurse. Because he had severe diabetic peripheral neuropathy he needed regular podiatric care. So we trooped to the doctor's office to have his feet examined. He and the doctor discussed previous hospitalizations for infected toes. The doctor turned to me and told me that I should check my father's feet every night to see if there were red streaks that might indicate a spreading infection. My father nodded in agreement. I could feel my nausea rising. So, as innocently as possible, I asked the doctor what would happen if an infection spread. He said it could be terrible and result in amputation. I looked at my father and then at him and said "Well, let's make an appointment to have his legs amputated right now, because if my father's feet don't matter enough for him to look for infection every day, they certainly don't matter to me." They looked as if the exam table had spoken to them. I said that although my father had no feeling in his feet, he was neither senile nor blind. If he saw something wrong he could call me. If I was out of town he could call a cab and get to the emergency room.

He actually did go several times to the emergency room and was hospitalized for treatment, but he died with both feet and all his toes. When he died I was physically exhausted and emotionally drained *and* he had had a good death and several happy years in a great city. I lived to tell the tale. This process worked because I had a care plan that accommodated my dad at his worst and me at my weakest. To do this I had to be honest with myself about his worst and my weakest. Facing these realities was the hardest part of the job, but doing so helped us stay safe inside The Caregiving Zone.

Little Deaths

"Would it not be better to give death the place in actuality and in our thoughts which properly belongs to it, and to yield a little more prominence to that unconscious attitude towards death which we have hitherto so carefully suppressed?"

—Sigmund Freud (Becker 1973, 11)

Death is often portrayed as a person: a skeleton in a black robe pictured in doorways or seen through a window carrying a scythe or riding a horse. It is often depicted as a being with the mission of selecting, gathering, transporting. In modern medicine death is described as an adverse event, almost an afterthought, of little or no interest to those who want to do *real* medicine. Over the years I've tried different ways of configuring death: as a medical event, an act of God, a law of nature. After all, I'm a modern, educated person. Death is necessary for life. However, I'm human. Death has taken too many of my loved ones. I hate it. It's the enemy I fight in my practice every day.

For me, death is an adversary. I fight for my family, my friends, my clients. I'm a big fan of second and third opinions and learning about new treatments. I go for anything I can find. I know I will always lose to this adversary, but not without a struggle. When the time comes my job is to surrender as gracefully as possible, but not a moment before.

I work with clients throughout the course of their illness, through acute episodes, plateaus and remissions, through the waiting times. I often go with them to medical appointments and procedures. We talk about issues and options. We process the ups and downs. The conversations are opportunities for healing and discovery.

Death is everywhere, all around us and in us. The processes of birth, growth and death shape our becoming. Our bodies are made up of cells and microscopic creatures that are constantly coming to be and dying. Death serves us in thousands of ways that make life possible. The immune system is a kind of grim reaper, moving through the body killing enemy cells and invaders. The idea of death being our servant, keeping our lives going, can be comforting. Having death as a constant companion is another matter.

There are two kinds of death: upper case and lower case. Upper case death is the last exhale. Each time I am present at a death I am amazed and saddened and often relieved. I am always amazed at the mystery of life as it comes to a close. There is great sadness at the truncation of any life; there will be no more opportunity for growing and learning in this body. To be honest, there is also usually relief at the cessation of a person's pain and suffering. If I've been the primary caregiver for weeks or months, I often feel relief that my job is finally done and I can get some sleep.

Lower case death is all the "little" deaths that precede the Big D: having to give up driving or the freedom to manage your own affairs; not being able to live alone; losing friends to death or abandonment; losing memory or the ability to walk. These little deaths can be as painful as Death itself. They need to be grieved. Anyone who has ever tried to get an elderly person to stop driving knows that Dr. Elizabeth Kubler-Ross's stages of death, especially denial, bargaining and anger, can apply with a vengeance to these little deaths as well.

In the normal course of aging and illness there will be many little, lower case deaths before the final Big D. These little deaths can signal the need for more care. This need sets in motion new ways of being and doing. Little deaths usually result in reduced abilities: small strokes might affect balance and coordination; macular degeneration can make it difficult to read; absent-mindedness can result in accident. Persons suffering these diminishments often struggle against their need to adapt to new behaviors like using a cane, having to be read to, or using a microwave instead of the oven. Maybe they've always been independent and now they see that independence steadily eroding. Family and friends are also faced with adapting to these reduced abilities. Adapting for them can be as simple as walking slower to keep pace or as complex as taking away the car keys.

These little deaths are always emotionally fraught. Newly disabled persons can be frustrated and angry. Those picking up the slack can be resentful, scared or sad. If the decline in a parent's or partner's abilities isn't matched with an equal incline in increased services, there's going to be a collapse sooner or later: a car accident, a fire in the kitchen, messed up finances, a serious fall, a medication mix-up. Less dramatic consequences such as poor hygiene, increased isolation and malnutrition undermine a person's health and well being over time.

Most of us will not die in our prime. We will be subjected to a variety of little deaths. How we adapt to new ways of being in the world is up to us. If we see adapting as *caving in*, as capitulation and failure, then each of these little deaths can be a major crisis. If we can see adapting as *acquiring skills*, then each of these little deaths can be viewed as a challenge to our resourcefulness and ingenuity. Sometimes adapting means acquiring new tools like a cane or wheelchair or life-alert button. Sometimes it requires negotiating for and accepting assistance with transportation, financial affairs and personal care. Sometimes it means moving to a more accommodating place.

In my practice I have often witnessed people confuse obstinacy with strength of character. One man had repeated fires in his kitchen because he wouldn't accept that his memory was failing and he needed to replace his stove with a microwave and an electric teapot. Another man insisted, despite his obvious weakness and lack of hygiene, that he was "fine."

Caregivers, be they partners or children or friends, also experience these crises. Mom's inability to walk might mean hauling around a wheelchair and lugging it in and out of the car trunk. Her forgetfulness can trigger childhood wounds. Dad's obstinate refusal to admit his need for help can propel the entire family into crisis management when he injures himself in a fall or is bilked of his money by an elder-abusing scam artist. Given that obstinacy is often backed by anger, tempers can flare, more harm be done and little accomplished. Family and friends may walk away saying "Well, we tried."

When I think of strength of character I think of people like Hilda who, despite occasional complaints about her failing body, has opened herself and her home to the wheelchair and commode and attendant care that she needs. Her days are rich in family and friends. They can visit knowing that she is cared about and cared for. Her (usually) gracious acknowledgment of her limitations and acceptance of appropriate assistance reduce everyone's burden of worry. Having known her for years I know how she has struggled to achieve this graciousness. Other faces come to mind—Katie, Alma, Rich, John. John was an expert paper-maker. He knew that as his HIV disease progressed his physical energy would decrease, so during the early years of his disease he collected all sorts of plant fibers and created a stash of beautiful art papers. When he could no longer do the physical work of papermaking, he would sit at his desk and make greeting cards and art objects using the paper he had made earlier. His foresight, planning, effort and courage circumvented a little death and kept him productive until the big one.

Death and the Body

It might seem self-evident that when we talk about death we're talking about the body, but entire conversations about death and dying can be carried out without ever mentioning the physical body. For example, one might discuss estate planning, life after death or grief and never mention the body. The fact is we will leave the planet over our dead bodies

As often as I've seen it happen, each death is unique. I find it helpful to describe the process as *deathing,* because of the many little and not so little deaths that precede the final exhale. Our bodies are birthing and deathing every moment of every day. Cells are born, live, work and die to maintain our physical reality as our bodies morph over time from newborn to toddler to teenager to adult.

We consistently underestimate how much life wants to continue living. I'm talking about the deep down organism-self that doesn't care about whether it can still read the New York Times or drive a car, balance a checkbook or look good for guests. At the organism-self level, each body expresses a life force that wants to keep flowing as long as it can

How many of us have looked at someone suffering from illness or severe disability and wondered to ourselves, "How is this person still alive?" To the life force, however, a body that is breathing is enough. The body can be described as containing worlds within worlds, a complex system of complex systems designed to sustain life. It has its own flora and fauna. It is equipped with food and waste processing facilities, tools for repairing itself, a sophisticated army to repel invaders, and complex mechanisms for interacting with and balancing to its environment. All of the body's systems are devoted to the business of living.

The process of deathing is the breakdown of these complex systems, until the organism can no longer sustain life. Sometimes this process is a cascade of breakdowns resulting in quick collapse. Sometimes the systems break down partially, but keep functioning at a reduced level. One can imagine somatic systems engineers working ceaselessly to keep vital operations going, even if all they can achieve is the minimum output to forestall death.

Why is it important to think about the body and its systems? The breakdown of these systems, intermittently or finally, can impact the dying person's daily life and his interaction with others. Breakdowns in the digestive system can result in difficulty assimilating food and eliminating waste, malnutrition, ulcers, diarrhea, constipation or gas pain. Problems with the nervous system can wreak havoc with organs and mobility and can also short out relationships. Over or under production of essential hormones can affect energy levels, sexuality and appetite. If the body's defense system is compromised, invaders have free rein. If the immune response is hyperactive, the body may turn on itself, attacking the thing it was designed to protect. The work of living with illness is adapting to temporary or permanent breakdowns in these systems.

Though these system breakdowns occur in a single body, their effects ripple throughout the web of relationships. Responding to these challenges, whether it's special dietary needs, problems with mobility, or a compromised immune system, requires lifestyle changes for everyone involved. The process begins with the sick individual adapting to the changes brought on by his illness and its treatment. As the situation becomes more complicated, coping strategies get more complex and more family and friends are affected.

It might be as simple as changing how the family eats, cutting down salt and sugar or eliminating allergens like tomatoes and wheat. Or it might require more extensive and expensive changes such as remodeling a home to eliminate dangers like stairs and sharp corners or widening doorways to accommodate a wheelchair. If the disability affects a primary wage earner, the changes required may be substantial and painful, affecting family finances and colleague workloads. Perhaps a partner will have to get a paying job. Maybe retirement will need to be postponed.

We know much about the nature and behavior of common disease processes. Much about these disease processes is predictable, even if there is no way to predict exact timelines and events in an individual patient. Every person's body will cope with system breakdowns slightly differently over time, but the general trajectory of a disease process remains reasonably predictable. Future breakthroughs in medicine may alter the landscape of disease progression, but the need for reciprocal and collaborative autonomy in dealing with the breakdown of physical systems will remain a cornerstone of compassionate care.

Death and the Brain

"...the mind develops at the interface of neurophysiological processes and interpersonal relationships."

—Daniel Siegel (Siegel 1999, 21)

We all received a crash course in death and the brain from Terry Schiavo, a brain damaged woman in Florida whose husband and parents clashed over whether or not to remove her from life support. People at bus stops and water coolers discussed the difference between persistent vegetative states and brain death. Politicians and religious leaders weighed in on the realities of neuroscience.

One sign that aging and death are approaching is a decline in mental powers. A diagnosis of Alzheimer's disease or another kind of progressive dementia can be unsettling and terrifying to an individual and his or her family and friends. People with diminished mental capacities may engage in covering behaviors like hiding their checkbooks. They can become enraged at even the smallest suggestion that they need some help with paying bills. But covering their behaviors leaves them vulnerable to mistakes like paying bills twice or failing to catch charges that aren't theirs. It also facilitates financial elder abuse and accidents in the home, like forgetting that the stove burner is on.

Speaking simply, we can describe the left side of the brain as being in charge of logistics. It deals with scheduling, computation, immediate memory and current facts. The right side of the brain takes the long view and is concerned with relationships, meaning and pattern. Illness temporarily slows down left-side functioning. Right-brain functions are in the ascendant. A sick person goes in and out of liminal time and space. A dying person lives there. They talk about meaning. Stories and memories are more important than facts. Touch, eye contact, a friendly face, shared humor and paradox become vitally important.

Modern life puts a high priority on left-brain functioning. Right-brain activities are pretty much consigned to religious rituals and the arts. Carl Jung suggested that the second half of life was the time for exploring what he called the *inferior function* (Jung 1956, 68*)*, aspects of the personality that had not yet been fully explored. Sometimes it seems to me that the development of left-brain func-

13

tions at the expense of right-brain abilities resembles a bodybuilder who only lifts weights with his right arm. Like bodybuilding, growing the mind requires balanced development. Coping with illness and dying also requires using the entire brain. We need the quantitative world of diagnostic tests, medication, and allocation of physical resources. We also need the qualitative world of the non-verbal and the non-linear to celebrate the essence that cannot be reduced to procedures.

Daniel Siegel, in *The Developing Mind*, writes: "As adults, we need not only to be understood and cared about, but to have another individual simultaneously experience a state of mind similar to our own. With this shared, collaborative experience, life can be filled with an integrating sense of connection and meaning" (Siegel 1999, 22). Entering into liminal space-time with someone who is dying enables this shared, collaborative experience.

I had only met Robby once or twice before getting a call one Ash Wednesday from his partner saying that he was bringing Robby home to die. He asked if I would help set up the apartment. After we prepared the apartment and got Robby settled, I went home having agreed to return the following day. When I showed up in the morning, the partner was inebriated and drinking straight from a bottle, as Robby, pumped up on steroids to control his lymphoma, was barking orders while teetering around the apartment. I knew right away that I was going to be there till the end. To prevent Robby from falling I had to keep him in bed. The easiest way to accomplish this was to engage him in conversation. I had no idea about his world or how to establish rapport with him, but at some point the conversation turned to Isadora Duncan. His face was transformed as he told me about her life and work. He was eager to make me love her like he did. I shared my own experience of passionate attachment to long dead heroes. We connected. He died on Easter Sunday.

I have many memories of connecting in this way. David and I could talk for hours about Nikos Kazantzakis. I learned from Randy the intricacies of purchasing Disney cartoon cels. Neil introduced me to the world of teaching gifted preschoolers. Elizabeth gave me insight into the world of prostitution and heroin. Michael and I met in our passion for the Trinity. A particle physicist allowed me to voice my thoughts about light and energy as life leaves the body. Tom explained to me the intricacies of the color wheel. Elaine revealed her vulnerability and let me and others make her last months, as she said, the happiest of her life.

Even as time is running out, there is time enough for sharing stories, for forming rapport, for discovering another person. To quote Martin Buber, "All real living is meeting" (Buber 1958, 11).

Communication

When people ask me if a client is dying, I know the expected answer is either yes or no. When instead I provide a decision-tree response describing various if/then scenarios, their eyes tend to glaze over and they ask again "Is he dying."

It's a pretty good bet that caregivers have little or no experience with the particular illness they are dealing with. Even if they have, there are significant differences between one person's experience of a particular disease and another's. There are hundreds of books and articles about the problem of misunderstandings in the workplace and the family, between men and women and between generations. They warn us that communication can be fraught with hazards. This is certainly true of caregiving as well.

Good caregiving requires nuance. It entails being sensitive to the person's illness, environment, and idiosyncrasies. Effective communication is crucial. But there are many potential obstacles to effective communication. Many people find it difficult to talk about themselves. This can be especially true regarding bodily functions. It can be equally difficult to *hear* about another person's bodily functions. Viewing the caregiving situation only as a series of problems to be solved as soon as possible can inhibit the process of hearing the whole story in context.

To paraphrase the Rolling Stones, you can't always get what you want, but if you try sometimes you get what you need. This is more likely to happen if you can distinguish between your needs and your wants. Successful interdependence requires dialogue. In the country called Illness dialogue is spoken in a whole new language called Bodyspeak. There is medical terminology associated with the diagnosis and treatment plan. There are ailing body parts and side effects. There is a lot to learn and a lot to say, much of it embarrassing. None of us was raised to talk easily about bowel movements or bodily fluids.

Many people don't know the difference between reporting and complaining. Reporting about one's condition is similar to the best journalism. It sticks to the facts; experiences of pain are described accurately with a minimum of drama. This is considered mature. Medical personnel appreciate this kind of communication because it is efficient and enables them to respond with minimal effort. Complaining, on the other hand, is personal and messy. It is often short on facts and long on emotion. It is considered to be less than mature and is dreaded by medical personnel who have little time or inclination to sort out a monologue.

What I find interesting is that usually I learn more from complaining than from reporting. Signals from body language, voice tone and prior similar complaints provide a richer picture. As I see it, we need *both* reporting and complaining to get the best medical care. The contents of complaints often hold vital information about what is happening to a person. The urgency of a complaint might also get more attention from medical personnel. Sometimes a cry of pain will get a faster response than a reasoned request for medication. Caregiver complaints can also generate action. One elderly client whose electrolytes were consistently off required several trips to the emergency room and frequent hospitalizations. I complained to every doctor we saw that she was vomiting every day. And, believe me, it was complaining: I had to clean up around the toilet. None of the doctors took my complaint seriously until we encountered a kidney specialist who said that the vomiting was causing the electrolyte imbalance. It turned out that the woman had a life-long eating disorder.

Having been on the receiving end of complaints from clients, I know firsthand how exhausting and grating this experience can be. I also know how frustrating it is to discover that someone I care about has been suffering in silence from a condition that could have been remedied relatively easily. Communication is essential to problem solving. Problem solving is crucial to caregiving and pain prevention. Hanging in there through the ups and downs of problem solving is a tangible sign of competent commitment.

It is a truism that some people want their problems solved and some people just want their problems. I have learned to stop trying when it becomes obvious that a person for whatever reason is attached to his or her problems. Psychologist colleagues have introduced me to the intricacies of primary and secondary gains, the very sophisticated and usually unconscious mechanisms people employ to get their needs met. For example, one man I worked with had almost quarterly health crises, some requiring visits to an emergency room. A life-alert button could have provided some backup. Moving to an assisted living facility would have gotten him immediate care. His sons were remarkably cheerful about it. I came to realize that these episodes allowed him to get attention and care from his sons on a fairly regular basis. The sons could express their affection in action. He received periodic confirmation that they would come if needed.

Sometimes it is a case of what Rosalyn Bruyere, founder of the Healing Light Center, calls *hardening of the categories,* a case of this-is-how-we've-always-done-it. We've always had throw rugs scattered around the house, so we'll continue to do so even if it puts mom at risk for a fall. I can't have another woman in my kitchen. I couldn't possibly ask for a ride to church. I would never hire a book-keeper to balance my checkbook. My daughter is the only one who knows how to take care of me. How much of this is fear-based? How much of it is due to an inability to adapt or a refusal to negotiate. Is the person unable or unwilling to negotiate?

Sometimes communication may break down because of faulty memory, resulting in escalating confrontation over conflicting remembrances. "I told you that yesterday!" "No you didn't; I would have remembered!" "I most certainly did, I was standing right here in the kitchen and I said..." After several rounds of sparring like this, a relationship can accumulate some serious scars. To forget a lot can be a sign of absent-mindedness or something more serious. Fears about losing one's mind often fuel an angry comeback of *you never told me.* It can be so much easier to make the other person wrong than admit fallibility.

Focusing solely on short-term problem solving can actually inhibit good communication. It can even be counterproductive if the problem being solved is really a symptom of something greater. For example, Parkinson's and Alzheimer's disease often cause paralysis of the throat muscles. Focusing exclusively on finding soft foods and encouraging the person to chew can be a way of avoiding the discussion about what's to be done when the ability to swallow is completely gone.

Problem solving can also be a way to avoid communication. I had one client who was hospitalized with several HIV-related infections. I was spending nights with him because of his care needs and the hospital's lack of staff. One night I was dealing with problems such as his IV line, questions about his meds, and the fact that his bed had not been changed. I was very much in my element, making things better, being vigilant. At one point he turned to me and said "I appreciate everything you're doing, but you haven't once made eye contact with me since you got here." I, of course, felt terrible and was immediately defensive. After all, I had just worked very hard to make him safer and more comfortable and I would be spending the night sitting in a chair looking after him. And then I realized that he was right. I was having a hard time looking at him. I loved him and he was dying. It was so much easier to bustle around and be busy. I sat myself down, looked him in the eye and wept.

Communitas

Doorways fascinate me. I love looking at photographs and paintings of doors. To pass through a doorway is to move from one space to another. Doors make it possible to enter and leave. Being diagnosed with a serious illness places a person at a doorway. One is in a place *between*, on the threshold of one's own death. However alive and well one might feel, the illusion of immortality has been shattered. Death has entered the house.

Caring for ill and dying people means stepping into a threshold world that coalesces around theirs. The writings of noted anthropologist Victor Turner provide some vocabulary and insight into this situation. In his book *The Ritual Process*, Turner proposed the concepts of *structure, communitas* and *liminal* to describe the processes of radical change in persons across their lifespans. All people cope with the complex challenges of adolescence, midlife, illness, dying and death. Turner studied the ways that different societies organize these processes to balance the needs of the individual with the needs of the group. One example is sending teenage boys off into the woods for initiation rites. I am sure that many parents today wish they could do the same.

Structure can be described as social stratification, customary behavior and patterns of authority. In contrast, communitas is freedom from these normative constraints, what Turner describes as "the liberation of human capacities of cognition, affect, volition, creativity" (Turner 1982, 44). The term liminal comes from the word *limen*, which literally means a threshold. A liminal person could be described as having left one place but not yet arrived at the next. For Turner, the terms liminal and structured describe different kinds of space and time.

A caregiver is a liminal entity, someone whose work falls between the boundaries of various professions and for whom issues of rank do not apply. He or she lacks the authority and influence that come with the title of doctor, lawyer, mother or father. That can be both bad and good news. Structured roles give us a sense of security. Who are we without a title? But the lack of formal structures makes it possible for new ways of being and relating to emerge. Liminal periods can seem chaotic, but they are rich in potential.

Turner describes a closeness that can develop among liminal folk, which he calls communitas. Drawing on the writings of Martin Buber, he describes communitas as "a flowing from I to Thou" (Turner 1969, 127). I have experienced this at times in the Caregiving Zone. It is probably the main reason I keep doing the work. Communitas happens when caregivers are able to function as equals, committed to a shared vision and values. Immense love can grow among those lucky enough to work this way, even though most volunteer work is one-on-one with the person needing service. Just listen in sometime on the stories that caregivers share with each other.

The caregivers I've teamed up with in the HIV epidemic have been accountants, lawyers, florists, doctors, psychologists, social workers, sales people and realtors. When they crossed the threshold into The Caregiving Zone, they too became liminal entities, performing the boring, sometimes odious and thankless tasks that medical service providers abhor and usually refuse to do. In providing comfort and companionship to a friend or family member they may have also healed themselves. I remember a priest helping me clean someone after a particularly noxious accident in bed; a mother and I giving her grown son a rectal suppository; a friend who had an important job with a university pulling over to the side of the road so our client could step out and vomit. Mostly I remember the times of keeping watch over someone with someone else. There is a moment in the course of performing a task when eyes meet and the world is changed.

Communitas also develops between caregiver and client, often in the form of play. I have many memories of playing with my clients. I remember David trying to teach me backgammon, but settling for beating me regularly at Scrabble. I remember Michael and I working on the Sunday New York Times crossword puzzle or going to see action movies together. I remember Allan and I throwing tapioca at each other. I remember Aiden driving me in his convertible with the top down on Highway 1. I remember George happily explaining to me the intricacies of the fictional airline he had created. I remember trying out new restaurants and walking through the rose garden at Golden Gate Park. I remember picnics and talking trash over coffee at Starbucks. And I remember laughing, lots of laughing. Laughing at bad jokes and puns, at the absurdities and indignities of life. Soiled diapers awakening the six-year old within, laughing hysterically about excrement. I remember jewel-like moments of tenderness that recreated us for another day.

Sometimes when I am sitting with a person who is sick I look at his or her face and, as I look, the face changes. Sometimes I see the lineaments of the child that was. Sometimes the outlines of a face can shift into a kaleidoscope of the faces of others with whom I have sat vigil. Every month of the year contains anniversaries of deaths. As I remember, a face will come to mind and with that face the faces of so many others with whom I have been privileged to work at the close of their lives.

Each face is like a snowflake, uniquely itself, even as it melts out of sight. The shape of each face is impressed on my retinas. If it is true that we retain the memory of everything we've seen or heard, then somewhere in my mind is the imprint of every face. Just because a snowflake melts doesn't mean it never was. Just because a person is gone doesn't mean we can't remember them as they were…unique…beautiful.

Hard, not Hideous

Dying is hard, but it doesn't have to be hideous. Dying is intrinsically hard but it is made even harder by pain and decreased personal sovereignty. It can become outright hideous if pain is left unmanaged or if the patient is treated like an object to be exploited and abandoned. One of the grimmest scenes I ever witnessed involved a young woman dying of a disease that had paralyzed her. She could not brush away a fly, get a drink of water or wipe her nose, let alone get to the bathroom. One of her friends approached me to see if I could arrange care for her while she was at work. I asked about the girl's family. They lived out of state and insisted the friend call social services to get help. We knew that she'd be long dead by the time social services came through with anything, if at all. I remember talking directly to her father and my inability to get across to him that she needed immediate professional assistance. He refused to pay for such care. In the end, her friend took a leave of absence to coordinate her care and to be with her during her last weeks.

The causes of a hideous death are many and varied, ranging from the gross to the subtle. They include lack of money, lack of compassion, and lack of good sense. I remember a dying man who tearfully begged his visiting mother to stay in town, knowing he would be dead in less than a month. She looked at him and at me and said it was impossible and besides, I would be there. I told her "I'm not his mother." She turned and walked away. Another man had a primary caregiver who wanted him to have a spiritually conscious dying process, so she banished all laughter and storytelling from his house and withheld pain medication for days. No one could talk her into compassion. He eventually tried to throw himself out a second story window. Common sense prevailed and he got the medication he needed.

Most of the hideousness I've witnessed has stemmed from wounded old relationships. My friend Francis really wanted to see his sisters before he died. He couldn't travel. Time and again his sisters put him off with some excuse: a child's communion, a graduation, work. He was holding on till they could come. One day he had a serious crisis and I spent the night with him at a hospital. When he woke in the morning and saw me his eyes lit up and a huge smile framed his face.

"You've come!" Then he realized his mistake and his face collapsed. "They're not coming, are they?" he said. From that point on he refused all treatment and let his disease take its course.

What prevents hard from becoming hideous is the availability of services and materials and protection from the predation of others. Being able to pay for services is one way to maintain independence in the face of encroaching needs. But what if the money runs out? What if there isn't any to begin with?

Dying at home can be incredibly low-tech. The only machinery involved is often a hospital bed and air mattress, oxygen equipment, and a pain medication pump. The hospital bed makes life easier for both the caregiver and the dying person. I do my best to encourage folks to get one because it is easier on the back of anyone who has to change the bed or provide personal care. Air mattresses prevent bedsores. Oxygen equipment facilitates breathing. A pain medication pump delivers a steady dosage with opportunities for the wearer to obtain an additional dose on an as-needed basis. If you can imagine having open bedsores or sitting with someone who is unable to get enough air or is writhing in pain, then you can see how essential this equipment is.

Now imagine being thirsty or needing to go to the bathroom, but there is no one to help you. Imagine calling out and no one is there to hear. Imagine your home filled with dirty laundry. Imagine that the pain medication you need is across the room but it might as well be on Mars. Addressing these problems doesn't require an advance degree. They used to be part of the job description of unmarried daughters. Now they're more likely to be performed by strangers as fee-for-service chores.

Those without money in this fee-for-service world rely on family or good friends or they hook up with a group of volunteers, patching together a care team. Often people start out with money and access to programs, relying on cash, insurance, or government-supplied services. But medical science and improved hygiene and sanitation have prolonged the lives of the chronically and the critically ill. Chronic long-term illnesses such as arthritis, diabetes, HIV and certain cancers may be punctuated with acute episodes like heart attacks, stroke and opportunistic infections. Medications and co-pays drain the wallet. People choose between paying for medications and heating their home or buying food.

Someday we all will need these services. How do we reconcile that need with our emphasis on independence and self-reliance?

The difference between hard and hideous is usually the *involved* presence of a *competent* caregiver. I stress the words involved and competent for good reason. People make the difference between hard and hideous, but not just any people. A caregiver needs to be involved and competent. Being involved means having a connection, a sense of responsibility for the person's well being, and a willingness to be responsive to the imperatives of the situation. Being competent means knowing what has to be done, the limits of one's knowledge, and where to go to obtain requisite assistance.

It is hard work to be an involved, competent other. Being in charge of someone's medication requires competent involvement. Competence is essential when describing symptoms to a nurse over the telephone or sitting, as I did once, in a derelict building in San Francisco's Tenderloin district where my only job was to protect my friend Mikey's barely conscious body from the rats. I met many involved, competent others while working in the HIV epidemic. Support groups like Shanti and The Zen Center, among others, trained volunteers and paired us with individuals needing everything from help with laundry to hospital visits. People used their spare time to run errands, clean, read aloud, etc. Whatever the task, their commitment reduced the two biggest factors in hideous: fear and loneliness.

What Time is the Next Stage?

In 1969, Dr. Elizabeth Kubler-Ross published her groundbreaking book *On Death and Dying: What the Dying have to Teach Doctors, Nurses, Clergy, and their Own Families*. She proposed her now famous five stages of dying: Denial, Anger, Bargaining, Depression and Acceptance. In her preface, Dr. Kubler-Ross writes that her book

> "is not meant to be a textbook on how to manage the dying patients, nor is it intended as a complete study of the psychology of the dying. It is simply an account of a new and challenging opportunity to refocus on the patient as a human being, to include him in dialogues, to learn from him the strengths and weaknesses of our hospital management of the patient..." (Kubler-Ross 1969, i)

Unfortunately her work *has* become a textbook and her five stages now dominate the discussions of both professionals and lay people who are trying to make sense of the dying process. Terms meant to make use of this new "opportunity to refocus on the patient as a human being" are often used as a form of accusation: He's still in the *anger* stage. She's trapped in *denial*. I hope he finally gets to the *acceptance* stage.

I should say here that I am not faulting Dr. Kubler-Ross. In fact, I came to respect her more than ever as I read her books again prior to writing this section. She came to her insights after lengthy interaction with her patients and reflection on her detailed observations. Interaction, observation and reflection led to insights which then informed her next interactions. Her books are not how-to manuals. She struggled to acquire a language with which to make her patients and their process visible. Her work invites us to observe and reflect on our own interactions. This means working with the person in his or her situation instead of imposing a one-size-fits-all program to resolve the crisis. I can see how the prior absence of a vitally needed language made it likely that her ideas would catch on so completely. But to be true to who she was as an explorer and thinker, we need to keep interacting, observing and reflecting.

Think of all the unique individuals from hundreds of different cultures, each with their own unique autobiography and complex dying processes, reduced to five words. By calling these feeling realities *stages*, we launch a whole juggernaut of expectations. After all, we are meant to move from stage to stage, aren't we? If there are five stages, then "success" is completing all five. Right? I don't think this is at all what Dr. Kubler-Ross intended. She was like an explorer returning from a far country who tries to communicate about what she saw there, knowing the available words can only point towards the experience, not sum it up once and for all. She wanted us to see the value in the dying process and how we could reduce much of the pain and loneliness. She also wanted us to get excited about the possibilities.

In my experience working with people in the throes of illness, aging, dying and death, caregiving is like solving a Rubik's Cube, one of those three-dimensional puzzles where the challenge is to line up each color on a side. If we imagine a Rubik's Cube, a six-sided square, we could name each side an area of concern: physical, mental, spiritual, emotional, relational, and financial. When we are well, we are able to cope most of the time with the realities and requirements of each of these aspects of being a human being. Our colors are reasonably aligned. Illness, dying and death disrupt this alignment and sometimes overwhelm our coping mechanisms. In every one of these areas of concern there are non-negotiable givens and there are variables. Much needed calm can result from sorting out a person's situation by areas of concern and then within each area discerning his or her givens and variables. From there it is possible to design a plan.

I suggest that we consider what's been learned about the development of the individual since 1969, such as how the child's mind unfolds, how family systems evolve, and the intricate neurophysiology of intimacy, memory and becoming. For example, Murray Bowen, MD, one of the most influential developers of family systems therapy, published *Family Reaction to Death* in 1976 (Bowen 2002, 321-335). Monica McGoldrick's video, *The Legacy of Unresolved Loss: A Family Systems Approach,* looks at intergenerational issues of grief and loss. She is also one of the authors, along with Froma Walsh, of *Living Beyond Loss: Death in the Family.* The work of psychiatrists John Bowlby and Mary Main, among others, explores the different ways children form attachments and the ways loss can affect an individual (physically, mentally, emotionally, spiritually) and the larger relationship network. Illness, dying and death are experienced and described in one way by the part of the mind that is linear, cause-and-effect, and fact-based and in another way by the part of the mind that is intuitive, metaphorical and relationally based. Separate cultures see illness, dying and death in different ways and have evolved corresponding customs and rituals to deal with them.

Dr. Kubler-Ross was studying people dying in hospitals at a time when the dominant trend was to do everything medically possible to keep them alive. Now we live in a shrinking healthcare economy with an ever-growing senior population. Many more people die outside of hospitals. Our discourse is more about rationing and physician-assisted suicide. Dr. Kubler-Ross made a case against doing tests and procedures on patients who were very near death, which can not only cause needless pain and suffering, but also so occupy the person that there is no time or energy for necessary conversations about end-of-life matters. The medical machinery is set in motion and can only be stopped with great effort.

But now the high cost of hospital care has sparked a movement to do as much as possible on an outpatient basis or with minimum hospital time. Cost-control conscious HMO's try to keep the number of tests and procedures to a minimum. The pendulum has swung very much the other way. At a recent conference put on by Kaiser Permanente, I heard one speaker say that twenty years ago the bulk of lawsuits filed against hospitals with regard to end-of-life care attempted get the organizations to *stop* treating patients who were near death. Now the bulk of the lawsuits are to *obtain* treatment if there is a chance this treatment could forestall the end. A person's advocate might be focusing more on getting treatment rather than stopping treatment.

Now that more people are dying at home, non-professionals are providing the bulk of the care under minimal supervision by medical staff. The good news is that the person is in a familiar environment, has access to friends and family and will not be subjected to fruitless testing and procedures. The challenge is how to construct a safe place to go through the end-of-life process and to facilitate the kind of conversations Dr. Kubler-Ross so valued.

Sometimes I talk to Dr. Kubler-Ross in my mind, especially when her now solidified ideas get used as a club to beat people. I talk to her about a client whose last words were "I am so angry." I suggest that this outburst was totally appropriate given that he was thirty-one and was a talented singer and dancer dying too soon of HIV. He died with integrity. He did not fail to complete his journey through the five stages.

Mystery and Logistics

"At the moment of utter solitude, when the body breaks down on the edge of infinity, a separate time begins to run that cannot be measured in any normal way…Is there not some fragment of eternity in humankind, something that death brings into the world, gives birth to?"

—Marie de Hennezel (Hennezel 1998, ix)

Death is a real. It cannot be prevented or avoided. Each person's death is unique. It is the ultimate *mystery*. Death also happens in a mortal body that is part of a relational network of family, friends, caregivers and service providers. It happens in a cultural context that dictates certain norms and limitations. It is a matter of *logistics*. If dying people and their communities of friends, family and caregivers are able to keep both the logistics and the mystery of dying in mind, they can craft scenarios that both challenge and support everyone involved with the goal of promoting synergy and healthy symbiosis.

Logistics and mystery are in play during the whole dying process, both before and after death. Logistics before death can involve everything from transportation to pain management. Keeping a person fed, clean and dry is a logistical challenge. Logistics after death may involve handling the body and taking care of final affairs. When a person is dying, the mystery of suffering is in the foreground. The mystery of eventual non-being looms in the background for both the dying individual and the community around him. After the individual dies, the survivors remain to cope with the mysteries by themselves.

Once doctors more or less handled logistics and clergy dealt with mystery. Given that many people no longer practice religion and have no affiliation with clergy, they may experience a mystery vacuum. There are various individuals and groups across the United States attempting to create programs to fill this gap. One problem can be that the people over whom the mystery of death is looming are hard-wired to an old faith and the new forms offered might not be weighty enough to counterbalance the dread.

Today there is a great hunger for the transpersonal. There are television shows about mediums, angels and the Divine in dialogue with a teenage girl. Surveys show that most Americans believe in life after death. Problems can arise, however, if mystery overpowers logistics. Too much emphasis on mystery, and medications might not be given on time or diapers not get changed. Beliefs about what lies beyond death, such as that the dying person is going to a better place, may result in things not getting done on earth as they are in heaven. Pain medication might be withheld to ensure the spiritual benefits of being awake at the final moment of life.

I once encountered a man sitting very serenely near the bed of one of my clients when I visited his hospital room. I noticed immediately that something smelled very bad. The urine drainage bag was dripping on the floor and had been doing so for quite a while judging by the size of the puddle. I went directly to the nurse's station to get some help and a chance to control my temper. I returned to the room and asked the serene gentleman if he had noticed the urine on the floor. He told me that he was there to sit with the dying, to meditate and to accept the situation exactly as it was. I reminded him that hygiene is important and pointed out that a urine soaked floor might not be pleasant for the patient or for visitors like me who could not rise above the environment. I told him that I was a student of medieval Christian mysticism, but I didn't want to live with medieval Christian sewage.

On the other hand, too much emphasis on logistics and caregiving can become rigid, almost fascist, excluding the sweetness and comfort that can come from acknowledging the mysteries involved. Some people do wait to die until a loved one can arrive. Holy Communion can sometimes ease physical pain. Sometimes more is needed than logistical care. When my friend Tony was in the hospital for an extended stay, none of the nurses on his floor spoke English as a primary language. They delivered their care largely in silence and spoke their own language among themselves. One day when I came to see him he started crying. I was the first person to speak English to him in three days. He told me he'd rather die on a street corner than stay there. He heard them talking and laughing and wanted in on the joke. "I feel like a thing, when they come in and do whatever they're doing and never look at me or talk to me," he said. His room was spotless. The bed was clean. His meds were coming on time. But he felt like he was in solitary confinement.

The fatigue of long-term caregiving can result in caregivers reducing people to problems to be solved rather than mysteries to be experienced. The punishing push to meet logistical requirements can dull everyone involved. That is why it is important to keep new people coming through the door, even though the impulse in most families is to circle the wagons or pull up the drawbridge. People are often glad to see me not because I'm special, but because I'm *new*.

Kairos and Chronos

In his book *The Present Moment in Psychotherapy and Everyday Life*, Daniel Stern describes Kairos as "a subjective and a psychological unit of time" (Stern 2004, 25-27). By contrast, chronological time, Chronos, is objective and measurable, a construct of consensus reality. We are all in agreement about the quantitative value of a second, a minute or an hour.

Yet how many of us have experienced moments that defied measurement? Minutes that seemed to pass like hours or hours that went by like a minute? How many of us have experienced a moment so overflowing with richness that it gathered our fragmented awareness into a particular now? It may have been triggered by a flower or a sunset or music. It might evoke a sense of being part of something bigger or of feeling the presence of someone or something outside of ordinary time.

Death is the end of a person's allotment of chronological time. We say of the dying that their "clock is running down" or of the dead that their "time ran out." For a person nearing death, consensus reality and its ally, Chronos, lose their exclusive hold on conscious awareness. There is more eternity in the day. There is more now in each hour.

Everyone in the vicinity is affected. Smells are stronger and more evocative. A glance can communicate everything that's needed. Small gestures set off waves of emotion. Being outside of linear time creates more space for stories and tenderness.

Moments of Kairos resist the technology of words and measurement. We use metaphor to describe them: "It was as if...The time went by like...." These experiences can't be precisely described or trapped by consensus reality. They can't be replicated. They can't be bought or sold. They are about revelation and form the ground of intimacy between two people. Kairos operates in the liminal realm, in the space between.

I think of all the time I've spent sitting with people, especially at night. Time can hang so heavy. Everything has been said. The second hand on the clock is doing its job. Sometimes there is the steady drip of an IV and the hiss of oxygen equipment. Sometimes I look up and the person is looking at me and it is as if I can see into their brain, can fall into their soul. It's as if I had never seen the person before. The moment passes and then maybe they fall back to sleep or need to go to the bathroom. We don't talk about what happened, but we are forever different.

We need Kairos to break the stranglehold of Chronos.

Values

Everyone knows the importance of the term *bottom line*. In accounting language the bottom line is the lowest line on a company's earnings report. What have we earned? What's the net profit? What's in it for me? In his book *The Left Hand of God*, Rabbi Michael Lerner describes how bottom line thinking has permeated almost every aspect of our lives: "...the bottom-line consciousness of the marketplace...assumes as a fundamental truth that human beings seek to maximize their own individual advantage without regard to the consequences for others..." (Lerner 2006, 73). People now often use the language of the marketplace in determining what is important to them. This is not all bad. It is important to be healthily pragmatic about logistics and Chronos. We live in a finite world. There are real limits to resources and time.

How then do mystery and Kairos figure in to the equation? What about important elements in human existence and relationships that cannot be quantified? What about aspects of our lives that cannot be reduced to line items on a balance sheet? What about expenditures of time, energy and resources that don't positively affect the bottom line? What about those that have a negative effect? How do we make choices we can live with? How do we make choices that others will have to live with?

Of course, we can choose not to think about it. Many of us unconsciously rush through our lives careening from one obligation to another, hoping, if we think about it at all, that it will all come out right. We might live with a vague sense of discontent or meaninglessness or foreboding, but the pressure of our days prevents this distress from erupting into conscious awareness.

Enter illness, dying and death. Mystery and Kairos enter into the world of logistics and Chronos. For previous generations, priests and doctors addressed these concerns while unemployed spinster daughters and cheap household help took care of the daily chores. Now we have managed medical care, limited religious influence, and a cash-based economic system that requires that almost every adult work outside the home. What happens to those adults who need daily care? What if they can't pay for services? What happens if we factor in mystery and Kairos as valuable, even if not income-producing, activities?

Illness and death can precipitate a clash between mystery/Kairos and logistics/ Chronos. It can be an intense confrontation. Division of labor in the family is an issue. Balancing work and home becomes even more difficult. Patients and caregivers will not be able to carry on with business as usual. What new activities and expenses will have to be factored in? What activities and expenses will have to stop, at least for the time being? How do we make these choices in a way that works for everyone in the family system?

I have seen family members take leaves of absence and even quit their jobs in order to be home to provide care. I have seen groups of volunteers put their lives on hold to provide around the clock care for people who had no one else to care for them. I've seen people provide full-time care, sometimes to the point that their own health was compromised.

Sometimes ill persons feel as if they are a terrible burden to those who care for them. They may need to be reassured that they are worth the sacrifices being made on their behalf. Likewise, caregivers may need to express their weariness and anger and to be reassured that they are making the right choices. Those requiring care and those who provide it need to ask what is important? Who is important? I always try to carve out time for discussions with people I'm working with about mystery and logistics, Kairos and Chronos. Most of the people I have worked with had done little prior work on values clarification before the current crises in which they found themselves. Many have appreciated being exposed to these ideas and an expanded vocabulary with which to explain to themselves and to others why they are making the choices they're making. Conscious living means being aware of one's available choices and owning up to the choices we make.

Our choices reflect what is important to us. Choices about life and death are crucial choices that say who we are. One meaning of the word crucial is *important or essential to resolving a crisis*. Illness and death are always crises. The process of choosing how to balance logistics and mystery, Chronos and Kairos, entails clarifying our values. Lives are at stake. No wonder tempers flare! No wonder people want to avoid these discussions as long as possible. Often it is only in retrospect that people can see what their values were. Maybe that is the up side of death as a constant in our lives. We get more chances.

Time and Money

Questions of time persist throughout illness, from diagnosis till death. How long will the tests take? How long to get the results? How long is the treatment? How long have I got? These questions remind me of the three Fates of Greek mythology: *Clotho*, the Spinner who spins the life thread; *Lachesis*, the Disposer of Lots who determines its length; *Atropos*, the Inflexible, who cuts it. How long is my life thread? What factors will determine its length? When will the moment come for my final exhale? And this person in the bed? How long is their thread?

Sickness, dying and death happen in real time. Life is suddenly interrupted. The interruption may come in a phone call or conversation. A family member or friend is sick, possibly dying. Sickness and death have entered the house. A new world presents itself, with new language and new ways of behaving, requiring specific skills. It is a moment in time when your life changes forever.

We use the same language for both money and time. There never seems to be enough of either. We spend and make time. We save and invest it. We want a return on our investment. How much time will I have to spend taking care of this person? How much time will I lose? What's the cost/benefit ratio? Are we talking about a trip to the store? Committing an evening to provide respite care? Spending an entire day at the hospital? Or are we talking about the potentially years-long commitment of caring for someone with Alzheimer's disease?

One's life and dreams are put on hold. There is the feeling that life is draining away, months and years lost forever. Control of time gets ceded to service providers and the dictates of the illness. The sameness of the days is often broken only by episodes of acute illness. The future looms as an endless succession of caregiving chores. Intellectually, you may try to remember that each of these chores protects and supports your loved one, but the terrible questions won't go away: When is it my time? Is this a waste of time?

Every illness has its own timeframe that sets the context for care. Much is known about the outworking of diseases. There is a lot of reliable information available about the stages of various illnesses and injuries and the estimated time frames for each stage. Having a sense of how much time is involved enables realistic planning. It is one thing to organize resources for an intense week or two and another to commit resources for a long siege.

To be able to allocate and manage time and resources well, it is necessary to distinguish between acute and chronic illnesses and injuries. Acute ailments, such as pneumonia or a broken leg, present different challenges than those posed by chronic conditions like asthma or Parkinson's disease. Acute conditions may be resolved by treatment and follow-up therapy. Chronic conditions become part of a person's daily life. At one time diabetes was considered to be acute and terminal. The development of insulin therapy converted it to a chronic illness with acute episodes. It is now the third largest cause of amputations in the United States. Opportunistic infections caused by HIV were also once viewed as being acute and terminal. But with the development of various methods of intervention in the HIV-virus reproductive cycle, HIV in the United States and other developed countries is now a long-term chronic condition, punctuated by sporadic acute episodes.

A distinction can also be made between acute or chronic conditions that are curable and those that are imminently or eventually terminal. Is it acute and curable like appendicitis? Acute and eventually terminal like pancreatic cancer? Chronic and long-term like Parkinson's disease? Are we dealing with multiple illnesses and intersecting timeframes? Many people, once past the age of sixty, will be juggling a variety of acute and chronic conditions. The daily management of high blood pressure, arthritis, circulatory problems and early onset diabetes might be punctuated by a mild stroke, pneumonia or a serious fall.

Acute situations produce a lot of adrenalin. We are pulled out of daily routines to organize a short-term mobilization of resources. There is often much drama involved. There is a story with a beginning, middle and ending within a relatively short time. Chronic situations, by contrast, are about immersion in the predictable round of daily life.

Money

Money is the joker in the deck of death and dying. It is almost impossible to talk seriously about sickness, dying and death and not to mention money. Money determines access to medical care. It is what will or won't remain when the person is gone. Every family has their own history with money. Family lore includes stories of success and failure, stories about having money and losing money. Family history about money interfaces with society's system of rewards and punishments for the haves and the have-nots.

Whether we like to admit it or not, we tend to quantify the worth of individuals in terms of their economic contribution to the marketplace. The sick, disabled and elderly may very likely not be earning money any longer and therefore may not be regarded as contributing much to the marketplace. But though they may not be earners, they are still spenders. When a person needs services but his or her ability to pay is in doubt, a crisis can ensue.

Perhaps a long illness has wiped out savings. Perhaps the person wants to preserve what is left for his heirs. Perhaps the heirs are averse to seeing their inheritance *squandered* on caregiving services. Perhaps family and friends have no money to pay for care. Perhaps no one is willing or able to admit how much care is required. Perhaps the individual wants to see if anyone cares enough to contribute without getting paid. Perhaps a serious health crisis comes on so fast that there is no time for negotiations.

Our social system is based on exchanging goods and services for money. It is a given that the supplier of the goods or services withholds them unless and until money is provided. But it is one thing to withhold a candy bar or diamond bracelet, and quite another to withhold critically needed care. Faced with the deep needs of the sick and dying, how do we negotiate a deal?

The word *negotiate* is perfect here. It can mean arriving at terms for a deal, reaching a fair and just balance of services and expenditures. It is also a term used to describe the traversal of difficult terrain, such as negotiating white water rapids. The environment is moving and risky for everyone in the boat. There's no time for haggling. Survival requires successful negotiation, staying in the present moment, and doing what has to be done.

Service providers are very clear about reimbursement. They provide clients with a schedule of services and associated fees. Payment is usually some combination of insurance payments and cash co-pays. What about caregivers? We can visualize the care needs of an individual as a large circle; call it the *Caregiving Circle*. The contributions of paid service providers can be represented as different sized circles within the larger circle. Everything else within the Caregiving Circle, the area surrounding the individual smaller circles, is the responsibility of caregivers: the daily chores and services that are not on the service providers' lists.

How do we put a dollar value on these services? If we did, how many people could afford it? How many would pay even if they could?

Caregiving has typically been women's work, usually performed by daughters and daughters-in-law. It was taken for granted and unpaid. If additional help was required, other women were brought in and reimbursed at the bottom of the wage scale. Spinster daughters often moved from one family situation to another providing care for the sick and the dying.

Women have worked very hard to obtain professional status and decent pay. The up side of this is that women are now employed as medical professionals ranging from doctors and physician assistants to registered and licensed vocational nurses and medical technicians in various specialties. The down side is that the services not covered by these professions, all the essential services not represented by the smaller circles inside the Caregiving Circle, still exist. They are generally not respected and are at the very bottom of the pay scale, if they are paid for at all. The sick, elderly and dying still need daily care. Who provides it?

In today's economy most adults work outside the home; some as a matter of choice, but more and more as a matter of necessity. We don't have the luxury of a supply of unemployed daughters and spinster aunts. Unfortunately, many people are still living in the past. If they have budgeted for home care at all, they might expect to pay according to the wage scale in use when they were young. Children might feel protective of their parents' estate. There can be a tendency to minimize the services that are required. After all, how hard can it be to make breakfast for one old man or to get mom to the bathroom or do a few loads of laundry? Laying out medications isn't so hard. Neither is driving to a medical appointment or waiting in line at the pharmacy. If the situation becomes more complex, requiring monitoring of blood glucose levels or giving insulin shots, how hard can that be? Family members may reason that if they were able to be at home they would be doing it all for free anyway, or that caregivers expect to be paid even when not *doing* anything at all.

Cash for care. No cash: no care. Who cares?

What does it benefit a person to get a new heart or new knees and then live in squalor or suffer from malnutrition? How do we have an honest conversation about the cost of daily care? Many families naively assume that Medicare pays for home care. Many families are less than honorable in negotiating payment for care and in keeping agreements. Home care providers have few protections.

I read recently that upwards of twenty million families are caring for elderly parents. Who is providing this care? Are they being reimbursed? At what level? Are we equating the amount of care we can give in our spare time with the amount of care that is needed? How big is the gap? What burden of preventable pain is being imposed? What violence is being done to loved ones who have to harden their hearts in order not to see the preventable pain, the dirt, the malnutrition, or the loneliness?

Pain and Suffering

Pain and suffering during the aging, illness and dying processes are both normal and in many cases preventable. Managing pain is a matter of logistics, of diagnosis and treatment, of using medications and technology. Pain and suffering are the endpoints on a continuum of intensity that applies to all forms of pain—physical, emotional, mental and spiritual. Any hope of successfully managing or preventing pain requires knowing what kind of pain it is and where it is located on the intensity continuum.

Physical pain can range from achy bones to constant agony. Emotional pain can run the gamut from momentary irritation to out-of-control anger and depression, perhaps resulting from unresolved relationships with family or friends based on misunderstandings or years-old traumas. Mental pain may come from worries about money or from the horror of losing one's mental abilities. Spiritual pain may stem from worry about old sins or it might be an all-out dark night of the soul. You need a varied toolkit to manage pain strategically. In addition to medications and technologies such as medication pumps and wheelchairs, you may need the tools and insights of psychology and the support and consolation of ritual and prayer.

To encounter pain is to encounter our limits. We don't just have pain. Pain has us. Suffering differs from pain. It is a mystery. Sometimes pain shades into suffering. Maybe the pain goes on too long. Perhaps pain joins forces with loneliness and becomes anguish. Exhaustion may lead to a downward spiral and leave a person feeling pinned and paralyzed like a mounted butterfly. Pain and suffering are often lumped together, which can mean that neither gets treated adequately. We speak of pain management, but I haven't heard anyone speak of suffering management.

Pain is often managed now by palliative care specialists. They use various technologies and methods to determine the source and to quantify the extent of pain. Is it nerve pain? Bone pain? Muscle pain? Referred pain? One can pick from a chart of faces illustrating various degrees of pain or indicate a number from one to ten. There is a complex pharmacopoeia of medications for treating pains of various intensity. How conscious do you want to be? How sedated?

Problems can occur when pain medication is administered outside of the supervised setting of a hospital. Patients at home may not take their medication for any of a number of personal reasons. They might say it makes them too sleepy or they fear becoming addicted. I've heard both caregivers and nurses express fear of being complicitous in addicting a patient. Often people allow their fears to overcome their judgment where pain medication is concerned. The difficulty of dealing with all the issues surrounding care for the very ill is magnified and complicated by untreated pain. This is another area where obstinacy can masquerade as strength of character. Caregivers are often hesitant to stand up for themselves in situations like this. In caregiving situations I ask people to deal with their pain honestly so the situation is bearable for me. If a person tells me that he or she can tolerate any amount of pain, I ask them if their families and caregivers can tolerate it.

Psychological and spiritual suffering, however, can't be treated with pain medications. I remember two women whom I assisted separately during their final illnesses who would howl for long periods of time. They would keen and wail, a long rise and fall of sound that would raise the hair on my neck. Their faces contorted like gargoyles. Both had severe metastatic cancer and both were very bitter. Both also had more than adequate physical pain medication. One of the women awoke from a sleep one day, smiled at me for the first time in weeks, and stroked my face. She was in a state of such happiness. She needed hardly any pain medication from then till the end. When she died she went out on a breath. The other woman was different. She keened till the end. During the last twelve hours of her life I read her psalms and poetry. A few minutes before she died her features relaxed into a kind of porcelain beauty. It was only after her death that I learned how duplicitous and angry she had been in her business and close relationships. Maybe those weeks of keening were her purgatory.

In my practice I see way too much preventable pain on every level. Sometimes the medication is sitting there but no one administers it. Sometimes the pain is misdiagnosed or mistreated. A person's fear of dying might be treated with an anti-anxiety medication alone instead of also providing counseling to address this universal human terror. Sometimes a caregiver's sadist shadow surfaces and extracts revenge for past wrongs. Sometimes physicians don't want to write a triplicate prescription for a narcotic drug because of possible complications with the Drug Enforcement Agency. Unfortunately there are few safeguards and second opinions.

People who work around pain and suffering develop a varied vocabulary to describe what they see. Many people just lump it all under the general term *unpleasantness,* to be avoided at all costs. Staying in the same room with pain and suffering is, for me, like learning to appreciate Bach's cello sonatas. I had to take the time to listen to them again and again before I could get beyond my initial dislike of the instrument and finally hear the music. Pain and suffering are integral to the human experience. They are linked to meaning. Immediately muting these realities with powerful drugs or shutting them down entirely through physician-assisted suicide might do more harm than good.

Physician Assisted Suicide

We are the self-help generation. We are also the generation of Caesarean sections. I know that some C-sections are necessary, but many are performed for the convenience of doctor and patient. The procedure becomes a way to control the timing of childbirth and circumvent the pain of labor. We are also the generation of garbage. From toasters to tires, we throw away and buy new. Lastly, we are the generation that watches survivor shows where people vote others off an island until they are voted off themselves.

These factors contribute to a mindset that makes physician-assisted suicide and the right-to-die movements so attractive to people our age. They represent *Control.* The Greek Fates are not for us. We wish to control our own fate. Control the timing and circumstances of our own death. Suicide is the ultimate fast forward. We design the end and then we implement it.

I know that the quality of care for the old, sick and dying in the United States leaves a lot to be desired. People often die in terrible, yet preventable pain. I know first-hand how exhausting on every level it is to care for someone through the dying process and how, at the end, one can feel as if there's nothing to show for all the effort. After the pain and messiness of birth, there's a baby to compensate for the pain and effort. After death, there's a corpse.

So why not just be an adult about it all and terminate ourselves before we are a messy, demanding burden existing at the mercy of others?

It's possible that in my lifetime physician-assisted suicide will become as acceptable a means of dying as Caesarean sections are an acceptable method of birthing. As is the case with C-sections, there may be little oversight. In the Netherlands there are procedures for medical oversight, but they are often ignored with impunity.

So what? Why can't people who want this kind of death be able to obtain it? There can be many up sides to the decision. A person with a terminal illness can avoid the suffering and indignities of the dying process. Their families and friends are spared the expense and effort of caregiving. The ability to schedule the death makes it easier for family and friends to be present. The individual is exercising his right to vote himself off the island. What could be the down side?

What about a person who gets voted off the island by his family or friends who might be unable or unwilling to provide the resources necessary to care for him through a protracted illness. He might be facing a choice between a family-sanctioned suicide or being left to the mercy of a rapidly disintegrating social service network. Due to the widespread use of amniocentesis there is now almost no support for families raising disabled children. They could, read *should*, have caught it early and thereby have avoided the whole problem. Will we also see no support for families taking care of members through a natural dying process? Why didn't he just kill himself and save everyone all the bother?

We are certainly not the first civilization to have to balance an aging population and available resources. Do we feed the eighty year-old or the three year-old? The three year-old is the future of the tribe. Does the eighty year-old have a special value for the group? However, we *have* the resources to care very well for our sick and our elderly. The problem is not production but distribution. How we ask a question shapes its answer. We can ask "Is it more humane to let a person take his own life rather than endure terrible suffering and indignities?" Or we can ask "Given that we have sophisticated pain management technologies and a growing understanding of illness and dying, how can we allocate resources so that everyone can live out their days in safety and security?"

In my experience the last months and weeks of a person's life can be incredibly rich for everyone involved. If we eliminate that time altogether, we cancel the possibility of something rare and wonderful happening. We lose the opportunity to be faithful and tender. These are not the kind of riches that show up on a balance sheet. Caregiving can be an incredible ordeal. So why do it? Maybe it's the endorphin high after a job well done. Maybe it's the satisfaction of being a member of a successful team. Maybe it's all the stories that get told by family and friends. Maybe it's the opportunities to make peace, heal old wounds and fulfill unmet needs, to be tender and loving. Maybe it's the bad jokes. Maybe it's because people aren't toasters

Affirming the importance of that time is my way of asserting the existence of possibility up to the last moment. Just because I can't see anything happening doesn't mean nothing is happening. Some family members have told me that they felt that the period of keeping watch had cushioned their later grief, as if the healing process already had been going on while they kept watch. They contrasted this with other experiences of loss that came at them suddenly with little time to prepare and that took longer to resolve.

I am very concerned about the long-term effects of assisted suicide on family and friends, not to mention our society and future generations. Physicians write the prescription and are then out of the picture. What about the pharmacist? What about the person who goes to the pharmacy to pick up the prescription? Who lays out the pills? If the person cannot swallow pills or is too weak to mix the concoction, who mixes it for him? Books like *Final Exit* (Humphry 1991) suggest putting a plastic bag over the person's face to ensure he doesn't wake up. Who secures the bag? Death is seldom instantaneous. Are people prepared for the deathwatch?

What happens to the person who performs these tasks? Immediately? Later? What about ancient taboos against matricide and patricide? What will be the consequences of violating these taboos? What about the family members who held the minority opinion? Did they get a voice? A vote? What will happen to the children and grandchildren observing this event? What decisions will they make about the aged and the weak? However we like to package euthanasia in the language of reducing pain, at its base it will always be about economics, expedience and efficiency. Will we have the courage to have honest open discussions about this trend?

Hope and Planning

Hope for the best and plan for the worst. That's it in a nutshell. People often tell me that they don't want to talk about dying and death because it kills hope or they fear it will worsen the illness or actually cause death. I have two responses. First I ask them if they have health, fire or theft insurance. Do they think that each time they pay their premiums they are causing illness or encouraging arson or theft? I then may suggest that I give them a few dollars to buy lottery tickets for me. If they are so powerful that they can cause illness and death just by thinking or talking about them, I want them to think and talk about my chosen numbers!

Sometimes *positive thinking* means *shutting out important facts*. Hoping nothing bad will happen is not a plan. Hoping for the best and planning for the worst are not contradictory processes. They can occur simultaneously. We hope the earthquake won't happen *and* we stockpile supplies in case it does. We hope that our tires won't go flat *and* we keep a spare in the trunk. We hope that our mom will recover from her stroke *and* we start talking about the day that may come when she won't be able to drive. We hope that the latest recurrence of dad's cancer is treatable *and* we talk to him about his affairs.

People have often told me that planning for the worst in cases of illness and dying is a kind of betrayal, a tangible sign that loved ones have given up hope. I counter that planning is a sign that everyone is giving up illusion, letting go of child-like magical thinking. Each of us is going to die soon or later.

What is hope? For me, authentic hope is the deepest affirmation of the potential for good in any situation, no matter how bad things might seem. Hope, however, can be used to paper over an entrenched refusal to look at the facts of a situation. It can also be a polite way to express concern but not real involvement. A pseudo-hoper will sound concerned: I hope dad recovers; I hope mom is okay driving at her age. If the reality is that dad has untreatable metastatic cancer, this kind of hope might be described more accurately as distancing, even abandonment. If mom has early dementia or problems with her reflexes following a small stroke, hoping it is okay for her to drive is a denial of the facts and the potential consequences to herself and others if she is in an accident.

41

Hoping is authentic when allied to active caring. The authentic hoper is a stakeholder. This kind of active caring can take the form of intervention: I hope nothing happens to mom, so I am going to do my part to ensure that she uses other means of transportation. Hope as active caring can also be a genuine offer of service: I hope you will let me help at this difficult time. I hope you know I am here for you.

What about giving a person false hope? We can get into trouble when we confuse hope with unrealistic expectations. Affirming the potential for good allows a space for complete remission *and* for a peaceful death. We can hope that catastrophe doesn't happen *and* know in our bones that there is potential for good in every catastrophe. Of course it can be a lot of work discovering that potential and bringing it to light. One way I discern between authentic hope and pseudo-hope is by the quantity and quality of conversation. Authentic hope promotes open-ended discussions. Pseudo-hope usually stops the conversation cold. Pseudo-hopers only want to hear the positive news. Pseudo-hope can obstruct organizing ways to cope creatively with bad news.

Sometimes the pseudo-hoper is a doctor who schedules a meeting or test with a client who is unlikely to be alive to make the appointment. I remember working very hard to get my friend Mark to start working on his end-of-life arrangements, specifically his financial information. His doctor was all cheery and upbeat during his last office visit and told him to schedule another appointment for six weeks. Mark seized on this as meaning he wasn't dying. Why else would the doctor be giving him an appointment? He again postponed organizing his financial information. He died four days later and we had to scramble for money for his cremation. The doctor had seen what I saw: a man in his mid-twenties wasted by HIV and lymphoma with critically low blood pressure. I sensed that talking about the future appointment in that upbeat tone was his way of distancing himself from his own sadness.

Pre-planning and paying for funeral arrangements can be one of the most generous and considerate legacies to leave to loved ones. It saves them from having to make many awkward and painful decisions in the post-death fog of fatigue and grief. There is nothing worse than scrambling to find someone's social security number or their mother's maiden name, looking through his or her papers just days after you've seen them breathe their last. Those times when everything was arranged beforehand and all I had to do was call the mortuary to pick up the body were a gift!

I recently did my own funeral arrangements. Given that I am always counseling people to do this, I thought I should *walk my talk*. It was not easy. When I mentioned to some of my friends that I had taken this step they immediately looked very concerned. They asked if I was sick. No, but someday I will die. Do I think that making my arrangements will hasten my death? No. Did the process of making my arrangements affect me? Yes. I spent two days in bed reading trashy novels with happy endings. The transaction was very sobering on many levels. My adolescent-self was confronted with real time. I also feel like I have taken care of my friends and family by reducing their workload with respect to cleaning up after I die.

Sometimes the consequences of poor planning can be horrific and hilarious at the same time. I had promised a friend that I would be with him when he was dying, so when I got a call from his partner in Santa Fe one Thursday saying that I should come, I bought a plane ticket and went the next day. His partner and I kept watch with other friends for three days, and then he died. We cleaned the body and sat with him for a little while and then I suggested that we call the mortuary to pick up his body. His partner informed me that he hadn't arranged for a pick-up because they couldn't afford the trip to the crematorium, which was in Albuquerque. We would have to drive him to Albuquerque ourselves in his van.

We were on the second floor and there was no elevator. I asked how we were going to get him down to the van. It was clear that no one had planned for this particular eventuality. Everyone had gone except for my friend's partner, myself and another woman, who promptly said, "I have a bad back." I was a short woman in her mid-forties who had been without sleep for 72 hours. My friend was over six feet tall. There is a reason it's called dead weight. I suggested, somewhat facetiously, that we sit him in a chair until rigor mortis set in and then the two of us could carry him down in a fireman's hold. We finally wrapped him in a blanket and, after several failed attempts, managed to lift him like a six-foot long sack of flour, maneuver him along the hall and down the stairs, stopping to catch our breath, and lay him out in the van in as dignified a manner as possible. When we eventually arrived in Albuquerque and backed into the loading dock, we were relieved to see that they had a gurney.

The conviction that we will be exempt from death is delusional. To my mind this kind of delusion robs the situation of its one saving grace: the opportunity to make meaning out of our collision with hard realities. Real hope generates momentum. Real hope affirms that we are strong enough to face hard tasks. Of course I hope that nothing bad ever happens to anyone I love. This is a given. I also know that I will bury everyone I love until someone buries me. This is also a given. Hope empowers me to work within the intricacies of suffering. Hope enables the seeds of possibility to grow.

While the exact timing and nature of our death cannot be predicted, there are questions we can ask and steps we can take to make the inevitable fact of our dying less fearsome and overwhelming. Where do you want your head to be resting when you take your last breath? Are you in a bed? On a couch? Is the bed in a bedroom or a hospital room? Is the couch in your living room? Who is standing around you? Do you want music and conversation or silence? Do you want prayers? Would you prefer to be alone or constantly companioned? The answers to these important questions can help you plan your last days.

Early in a woman's pregnancy, medical staff will ask her where she plans to have her baby. She might want a home birth, but her physician might suggest a birthing place with more access to medical equipment and expertise. The woman is encouraged to visit the birth center and think carefully about her options in the light of what is known about the specifics of her pregnancy. There might be potential complications that would be handled more easily in a medical facility. No one tells her that she shouldn't be thinking about the birth because such thoughts might jumpstart her labor and delivery. No one suggests that she wait until her water breaks to choose a place to give birth. No one tells her she isn't pregnant.

Denying our death and expecting everything somehow to turn out all right in the end reminds me of those scenes in movies where babies are born in taxicabs. The woman is in pain. Well-meaning, but untrained strangers are called upon to assist in the delivery. We hold our breaths and wait for the infant's cry. Eventually a smile breaks on the woman's sweat-stained face and the cabdriver gets a kind of ah-shucks look. The ambulance arrives and all is well. But in reality we do not deal with women giving birth in cabs by making emergency medical training mandatory for cabdrivers. We don't insist they have layettes in the trunk. We try instead to provide prenatal care so that births in taxicabs are the exception. We know that birthing in a taxicab is dangerous and puts the mother and child at risk.

There are times when death comes without fanfare. A person dies quietly in a chair. There is an accident or a sudden illness: a taxicab death. The rest of the time there are lots of signs that death is not just in the house but is sitting at the bottom of the bed. Unlike the case with pregnancy, we cannot predict a date of death. However this doesn't mean we don't know a lot about how a person will die of a given disease and how the dying process will unfold. There are identifiable events that mark turning points from which there is no going back.

The most common question asked upon diagnosis with a potentially fatal illness is how long do I have. As a rule the only prediction doctors will make is the "less than six months" required to qualify for hospice services. Sometimes they will narrow it down, but not often. Nor should they. People have amazing survivability. I have seen individuals last months when the doctor predicted days. I usually suggest that family and friends plan for *both* a quick death and extended care. If they think they have months and it turns out to be days, they might not have a chance to be there. If they think it is hours and it turns out to be months, the roller coaster ride can be exhausting as the dying process becomes a scramble for resources. Fatigue threatens to swamp feelings of love and devotion.

Having a vision of your last days and hours can shape your plan. Sharing that vision with family, friends and care providers can ensure that your head will be resting where you want it when you experience your last exhalation. Facts are your friends. Just because we don't know everything doesn't mean we don't know anything. Whatever our illness or disease, there is a good chance that others have died of it. The facts are out there.

Facing Fear

Much of being an adult comes down to "never let them see you sweat." We learn to hide our fears at a very young age. In later years perhaps we seek treatment for phobias or opt for anti-anxiety medications. But all this is private business. There is a lot to fear in the land of illness and dying: pain, disability, all the little deaths that precede the Big D. Fear can worsen pain. It can interfere with problem solving. It can make you rigid when it would be more helpful to be flexible. I know that fear makes me very crabby.

Fear-based behavior can put intolerable pressure on relationships, both public and private. I have known two situations where patients with terminal, though not yet critical, illnesses divorced their partners. I was stunned in both cases. The well partner in each instance had been an exemplary caregiver. What was going on? In both relationships the person who was sick could not live any longer with their terror that the loved one would leave when things got really bad. As one woman put it, her fear of being abandoned was greater than her fear of dying alone. Waiting for his (what appeared to her) inevitable departure was an intolerable strain.

Can we create a working relationship with fear? What beliefs do we have about fear? Is it unmanly? Immature? Just another emotion? Is it possible to recognize fear as normal and valuable and to learn skills to cope with it? Fear is a given in the land of illness and dying. It isn't going to go away.

One technique many people use is to get angry. Running fear on the anger channel is more socially acceptable; it makes you look in control. It can seem more adult to be angry or at least to have an angry edge to your speech and actions. I grant that anger can sometimes be effective. The adrenaline can provide energy to break through fear and paralysis. The problem is that this energy can be expensive; it comes at a cost. It can leave a lot of collateral damage and a trail of broken relationships in its wake. Sharing our fears is risky. How will we be treated if we show our vulnerability?

When I begin working with a new client I always ask the same question: what are your three worst fears? The answer is almost always the same: I'm afraid I will be in pain; I'm afraid I will be alone; I'm afraid I'll be dirty. I do my best to reassure the person that pain can be managed, that someone will be there, and that every effort will be made to keep his or her body and surroundings clean. From there we may move on to other fears: fear of needles, fear of being ripped off, fear of being humiliated, fear of dementia.

The experience of illness and dying can bring about a crisis of fear. Defenses formed over a lifetime can begin to crumble. Many people were raised in frightening circumstances. Perhaps they learned to be afraid before they learned to walk or speak. Repressed fears may resurface. Experiencing the process of illness and dying, whether it's our own or that of a friend or family member, can be a great opportunity to learn new ways to live with fear. Much of our lives is spent in fear. We are afraid for our jobs, our pensions, our children, our health. Dealing with the fears of the dying can be a chance to address our fear. There are people who have survived serious illness or a near death experience and have described it as liberating and energizing. Many say they now live without fear.

Several years ago, I received a call from the secretary of the church I was attending in San Francisco. She asked me to visit a man named Dennis who was hospitalized with HIV infection. I'd had never met him, but he had heard about me. I thought he wanted a massage, so when he asked me what I did I started talking about the benefits of massage. Suddenly he sat up, threw his spindly legs over the side of the bed, pulled off his oxygen mask and shouted, "I don't need a massage! I'm dying! I don't know how to die. People told me you could tell me what to do."

I switched gears and we talked a bit about his physical condition and then I asked him about his fears. He said he was terrified that he would die alone since he had many acquaintances and no friends. I told him that one way or another I would make sure that he was not alone from this moment till he died. He then expressed his fear that he would die without talking to his family with whom he had been estranged for many years. I asked him if it was okay to call his family and tell them what was happening. He said yes and I called the church secretary and gave her the number. While he and I were talking he received a call from his sister. In the course of that day he talked with everyone in his family. Later one of his brothers flew out to be with him. His last concern was paying for his funeral. He told me how much he had and a friend of his agreed to make up the difference.

During the next few days I stayed with him during the nights and his brother covered the days. His friends came and went. Dennis moved deeper and deeper into peace. After about a week it was clear that he was approaching the end. During the last night of Dennis's life, his brother stayed and we kept watch together.

At one moment he opened his eyes, looked at me and died. No fear. No struggle. He had not been alone since our first conversation.

I don't know how to get across how wonderful it is to be able to accomplish something like this for another human being; to meet fear head on; not to eliminate it, but to be able to prevent the feared worst-case scenario. Of course, it helped that Dennis was very clear about his worst fears. In my experience most people are very clear when death is lounging in the corner of the sickroom. There is something blessed and terrible happening when someone shares their fears. It is so intimate. I feel honored when a person trusts me to that extent. I take it as a call to action, an opportunity for discussion and crafting a plan.

Grieving

Anthony was the first person with HIV/AIDS for whom I volunteered to do massage and provide whatever emotional support I could during what turned out to be the last eighteen months of his life. It was 1991 in San Francisco and Anthony had been doing his best to cope as HIV/AIDS decimated his community. Even though he was struggling with his own illnesses, he volunteered as a caregiver and counselor. He took me under his wing. Our massage sessions were as much about his tutoring me in the realities of the epidemic as my trying to provide him with some relaxation and pain relief.

One day he asked me how many of my clients had died during my twelve years as a hospice volunteer. I told him five. He asked me how many of my clients had died in the year or so I had been working with people with HIV/AIDS. I said ten. He stared at me intensely but, as if talking to himself, he said that the loss of ten people marked a watershed; another was when you reached the twenty-five to thirty mark. Then there would be a crisis at the fifty to sixty mark and another as the tally approached one hundred. He wondered aloud if I would still be around as the numbers of the dead increased. I remember looking at him in absolute horror. Of course he was right. In San Francisco in the early 1990's death was everywhere. One summer I lost twelve clients in fourteen weeks.

Grief is as unique and idiosyncratic as the person experiencing it. It is physical, emotional, intellectual and spiritual. In reaction to a terrible loss, grief can encompass a wide range of feelings, including relief. The shock of grief is proportional to the newness of the experience of loss. The loss of a loved one can be experienced as an unanticipated assault. There is fear and anger mixed in with the sadness. Death is an affront. We have been disturbed. We were not consulted. Experiencing numerous deaths in a short amount of time shatters any illusions that death is a *thief in the night* or a terrible anomaly. Shock and awe give way to a deeper and more private accommodation

It has been very helpful for me to know people who share this level of loss. We have great patience with the unique ways that each of us copes with the outworking of grief. We have patience for grief's duration. There is a difference, I think, between unresolved grief and living every day with the Mystery of the loss of a loved one. Too often in our society today, past a certain point, there is little patience for the outworking of grief. The process is messy and unpredictable.

I feel as if my memories of my dead are now part of my DNA. My memories of them interact with all the other people and things jostling for my attention. We may try to sequester memories of loved ones in a kind of solitary confinement, as if amnesia or silence can heal grief. But memories are cellular and alive. They are woven into the fabric of our daily lives. As long as we remember them they are not dead to us. Grief is not necessarily a pathological failure to consign the dead neatly to the past. Grief is an essential component in the maturation of an individual. It is crucial to learn how to grieve. We can become attuned to the rhythms and cycles of our own grieving.

Grief is so intensely personal that it is hard to come up with norms. What are the signs and consequences of healthy grieving? Of unhealthy grieving? How much of the outworking of grief is determined by culture? How is it different now from our parents' and grandparents' generation? My first example of unhealthy grief was that of my mother for her dead father. Even at the age of ten I had a sense that there was a lack of proportion to her grief. She had never gotten over her father's death. It remained a hot button issue for her. She would express tearful memories and anger at her mother and sister more that twenty-five years after his death. In a very real sense my mother's life stopped the day her father died, like Mrs. Haversham in Dickens' *Great Expectations* who was jilted on her wedding day. Living in her memories and decrepit wedding dress, she is steeped in the bitterness of the rejection and the death of her hopes. Life has moved on but she cannot. I used to think that with age and enough personal growth and development the bitter and the sweet would blend into a palatable concoction. I find instead that as I get older the bitter gets bitterer and the sweet gets sweeter. I have somehow to make peace with both. I think this forms the basis for healthy grieving.

Displays of grief can be disturbing to witness. Underlying our efforts to comfort is a desire to get everything back to normal as quickly as possible. It is hard to be around pain. It is especially hard to be around pain that doesn't seem reasonable to us, that seems out of proportion to the actual loss. There are folks whose loss is so traumatic that they cannot risk that kind of hurt again. They do not have the resilience to take the blow, suffer the hurt, withdraw to recover, and then reemerge to participate again in affairs of the heart. Religious belief may increase resilience for those who believe in an afterlife and a final reunion with loved ones.

I have learned a lot from the partners of people I've cared for until their death. Their grief took them out of the mainstream for a time, but they came back. The grieving process is like a branch of a river with its own landscape and challenges but leading eventually back to the mainstream. Unhealthy grieving might be described as swimming against the flow in one of those tributaries, resisting the current that will bring one back to life, to a new place in the stream. One man who had lost his beloved wife told me that he cried one day because his toast had tasted so good that morning. It was the first time since her death that food had tasted good. He felt relieved and a bit guilty and sad. He said, "Now I know she's gone." Another man I know struggled for sixteen years with the mystery of his grief at the death of his partner.

It makes sense that we would be ignorant and inarticulate about grief. We are ignorant and inarticulate about death, which gives rise to grief, whether it's the death of a person, a marriage or a way of life. The key to resolving grief is to take into account the landscape and conditions of the stream of grief in which we are swimming. For some, grief will be a brief time away. For others, like my friend, it's can take years. Listening provides insight and love gives us patience with our grieving friends.

Predator and Prey

When we watch a nature program about lion cubs carefully nurtured by a devoted lioness, we might cringe a bit when she drags a baby antelope home for dinner, but our hearts go out to the lion family. They need to eat. Or perhaps we watched a gazelle give birth on the savannah and held our breath until her foal stood, nursed a bit and began clumsily moving with the herd. Perhaps the presence of lions, hyenas and vultures on the periphery increased the tension. We know the consequences for a baby that can't keep up with the herd. We watch sadly as the old buffalo is brought down by lions hunting in tandem.

We can relate to the needs of both predator and prey because we are both predator and prey. Our hunger moves us to hunt. We are hard-wired to recognize prey: those who are physically smaller and weaker, the vulnerable, the strays and the old. We may not prey on our fellow humans as the lion does on the gazelle, eating them to sate our hunger, but we might hunger for their money, medications or property. We might need them as objects on which to vent our frustrations.

This hunger for possessions on the part of caregivers can stem from sentiment, such as a desire to have something that belonged to a loved one. Or it can be a hunger for something desired but not readily attainable. Sometimes it's a hunger for retaliation for putting up with daily insults. Sometimes it's a hunger for reward, like adding a few groceries for oneself to the shopping cart; consider it a surcharge or a supplement to low wages.

The family of one of my clients came in from out of town to keep him company until he died and after he died they sat around waiting. They assumed his Will and Testament would be read the very same day. They had brought packing materials, just in case. Another family drove in from out of state and rented a van the day of their son's memorial. Prior to the service, they stripped his apartment of everything of value. They departed directly after the memorial service, not saying a word to any of us who had taken care of their loved one.

The predator in us may not be restrained from preying by ties of family or friendship. Abuse of elders is usually perpetrated by family members. I know personally of situations where people got their parents to co-sign loan papers while they were coming out of surgery or undergoing heavy chemotherapy. Hospitals and nursing homes display signs saying they are not responsible for theft. Who steals from people in hospitals and nursing homes? Do patients steal from other patients? Perhaps. But it's more likely that staff and visitors steal from these weak and vulnerable people. They can be robbed of possessions like tape players, articles of clothing, medications with a high street value, even soap.

Are the people perpetrating these offenses like vultures chewing on the carcass of a dying zebra? Like the lioness trying to feed her cubs the only way she knows how? Can we see how the person in the bed resembles an aged wildebeest circled by lions slowly moving in for the kill? Can we imagine how the elderly woman who lives alone is systematically overcharged for or sold unnecessary home repairs.

We tell ourselves we are higher than animals. When predatory behavior occurs we are stunned, speechless, appalled. Confronted with crimes against the vulnerable and the ill, we protest that they should have protected themselves. We hang signs in hospital rooms warning people who are sick and scared that there is a high probability that they might be robbed on the premises.

I remember visiting the home of an elderly dying woman as part of a care team only to find that her home had been completely stripped of every item of personal or economic value. It looked like she was in the process of moving. There were marks on the walls where pictures had been. There were no dishes, no towels. Her family had expected her to die in the hospital and had seized their opportunity. We requested that they at least bring back some pots and pans and dishes. The woman cried for her missing photos and curios.

The news is filled with stories of predators: counterfeit drugs are sold on the Internet; a pharmacist waters down his customers' chemotherapy drugs. When I stay with someone in a hospital, I always check their medications before they take them. Sometimes there are honest mistakes. But sometimes hospital personnel steal medications to sell them on the street or to sate a habit. Sometimes a patient is given Ibuprofen instead of the prescribed Vicadin or morphine. The street value for these drugs is very high. Then, of course, there's the predation of marketers using advertising to convince you that you're sick and need to take their drugs.

For the most part, animals avoid the sick and dying except as a food source. We describe animals going off to die, but it is just as true to say that the troop leaves the frail behind. The impulse to move away is based on survival instinct. In the wild, those that lag behind are certain prey to hunters and scavengers. To stay with them is to become prey as well.

Given that most of us run on instincts, we find all kinds of reasons not to visit the sick, or we stay for ten fidgety minutes and then flee. We don't wish to become prey ourselves. I know that sometimes I have to sit on the steps outside for a few minutes to overcome my resistance. Maybe this is why most spiritual traditions strongly suggest caring for the sick and the dying. To the extent that a spiritual practice requires the awareness and modification of instinctual responses, the charge to visit the sick brings all this material up for review.

It can be profoundly uncomfortable to discover the predator within. Seeing another person so vulnerable can awaken very primitive anxiety. I am more understanding of how difficult it is to show up when someone we know is sick or dying. We always have so many other places to go.

Across cultures, people wish to be safe and secure in their body, mind, emotions and spirit. This need is preverbal, coded into the deepest layers of our body/mind. Attachment theory in psychology tell us that, unlike reptiles and species of mammals that run to the nearest cave or up a tree, humans are hard-wired to run to other humans when threatened.

Being sick and weak exposes us to all sorts of dangers. Seeking a safe harbor in another person can also expose us to all sorts of dangers. Our process of finding someone will be affected by our personal history with Safe and Secure. Yet as popular songs attest, we keep searching. George Gershwin put it succinctly: "…oh how I need someone to watch over me."

Humans are both predator and prey. We are also providers and protectors. Perhaps your vulnerability gives me an opportunity to express and explore not just the predator-me, but also the provider-me and the protector-me. Together we can create new experiences of Safe and Secure.

I have spent many days and nights with people who needed someone to watch over them. Sometimes in the night I have felt part of an ancient lineage. At some point in our evolution, humans broke out of the predator/prey dichotomy and began to care not just for our children, but for the old and the sick as well. We risked becoming prey by helping prey. We learned to be around prey and keep a leash on our predator. Eventually we learned to channel the predator into the protector.

Predator. Prey. Protector. Provider. In every caregiving situation all of these players are present. It's not about the savannah and lion prides and wildebeest. It's not about hunting and being hunted. It's not about scavenging after the leavings. It is about keeping the caregiver shadow at bay. It is about safeguarding against medical mistakes and hungry scavengers. It is about stopping the pretense that no safeguards are necessary.

Independence

Americans are big on independence. We fought a war for independence. We celebrate Independence Day. We have icons of independence: the lone cowboy, the entrepreneur, Horatio Alger. Ask almost any adult about his or her primary concern about aging and illness and the answer is usually "I worry that I will lose my independence." People who continue to drive a car long past the point where it is safe and financially feasible to do so claim they "don't want to be dependent on someone else." Often we shudder when we look at someone who is, by our definition, dependent. We wonder how they tolerate this state. People have told me they would rather die than be dependent on anyone for anything.

What is it about being dependent that makes it a fate worse than death? I suggest it is a variation on the predator/prey dilemma. To be dependent on another person is to be powerless. The degree of dependence determines the level of powerlessness. Even the anticipation of being powerless triggers our fear of being helpless prey. I can see why having a car is so important even if a person is too old or sick to drive it. It affords the means to flee.

Independent equals adult, predator, sufficient, strong, dominant and able to defend one's territory. Dependent equals child, prey, needy, weak, dominated and vulnerable. Who would ever want to be dependent? All around us are examples of the negative consequences of being dependent: examples of outright abuse and all the lesser insults dished out by those who have the upper hand. No wonder people describe it as a fate worse than death. Still, the fact remains that throughout our lives, and especially at the end, we do need others. We become weak and vulnerable.

Does it automatically follow that we have to fear becoming prey? What if we described the situation differently? Instead of seeing dependency as an all-encompassing *state*, what if we saw it as being conditional? Perhaps I can make my meals and clean my house independently, but I need help with transportation getting groceries and going to church.

What I am trying to point to here is the tremendous amount of fear that often prevents this kind of discussion and negotiation. People can feel that to admit to the slightest need for services means the end of personal sovereignty. I've seen individuals suffer isolation and malnutrition and even leave illnesses untreated, rather than risk letting someone see their weakness.

Sometimes I can get a person to talk about his or her experience of the dark side of dependence: what happened to them as a child, what happened to the elderly in their family. Sometimes I can get a person to talk about what he or she may have done to others who were dependent and who now fears it coming back around. Sometimes it can be possible to create new experiences. Sometimes people would rather die.

Are there alternatives to the independent/dependent polarity? One ethicist, Anne Donchin, suggests "a relational concept of autonomy" as a way to describe the individual embedded in a network of relationships encompassing a range of power-dynamics, rights and responsibilities. The idea of relational autonomy provides a multi-dimensional context to discussions about giving and receiving needed care. Professor Donchin describes relational autonomy as being reciprocal and collaborative, involving "a dynamic balance among interdependent people who are engaged in overlapping projects" and "an appropriate respect for personal autonomy." Such respect requires "those in positions of responsibility...to respond sensitively to the experiential world of those in their care, to deploy their power and influence to restore and strengthen the autonomy of those they care for, and to support their struggles to create new personal meanings out of the experience of disease, disorder, and disability..." (Donchin 2000, 191-92).

In this context, for example, the desire to drive in order to maintain independence in spite of disabilities would be balanced against the risks to others on the road. Others in the relationship network would take both of these factors into account and assist the person in making self-respecting arrangements for transportation, staying sensitive to the person's fears, while also asserting the rights of other drivers and pedestrians to be safe.

The Caregiver Shadow

"Particularly when a case worker is forced to operate against the will of the person concerned, careful analysis of the depths of the unconscious reveals the power drive as an important factor. In general the power drive is given free rein when it can appear under the cloak of objective and moral rectitude. People are the most cruel when they can use cruelty to enforce the "good."

—Adolph Guggenbühl-Craig (Guggenbühl-Craig 1971, 8)

In the quotation above, Dr. Guggenbühl-Craig is describing social workers, nurses and therapists, but the same power drive he describes is activated in any caregiving situation, especially in the private home where there is hardly any supervision or feedback. He writes, "the greater the contamination by dark motives, the more the case worker seems to cling to his alleged 'objectivity.' In such cases the discussion of the actions to be taken in a case become blandly dogmatic as if there could only be one correct solution to the problem" (Guggenbühl-Craig 1971, 8).

Very little is written about the caregiver shadow. In the media caregivers are treated like traditional mothers, wrapped in sentimentality or ignored altogether. They are often described as stressed-out and heroic, so we are shocked and appalled when tales of abusive caregiving are thrust into our awareness.

I have seen caregivers insist on waiting an additional ten minutes to administer medication, even though a sick person is writhing in pain, because that is what it says on the prescription bottle. I have seen caregivers withhold pain medication altogether, citing their fears that the person in the bed will become addicted. I have seen caregivers force food down the paralyzed throats of people unable to resist, because the doctor said they should eat. Several of these situations required performing the Heimlich maneuver to release the food stuck in the person's throat. I have seen caregivers prevent visits from a patient's family members and friends because they claim that visitors are exhausting or upsetting to the person. The patient becomes increasingly isolated and easy to control. Caregivers can wrap their darker motives in "the cloak of objective and moral rectitude."

Dark motives can also insinuate themselves into discussions about logistics. I always become alert when a primary caregiver insists that there is only one way to organize care, only one way to arrange the schedule, that only he or she can provide the necessary care. Sometimes it is a spouse who finally has the upper hand or a daughter sitting on years of rage. Power can be quite heady if a person has felt powerless for most of his or her life.

The caregiver shadow can emerge with a vengeance when dealing with toilet issues. If the primary caregiver is a son or daughter and the person receiving care is the mother, I always ask her about family toilet training. Is there anything we should get out in the open given that the people she once toilet trained are going to be assisting her? Grown children can be completely unaware of the feelings of rage and shame they carry around until they are suddenly faced with the problem of an incontinent mother. There is a strong likelihood that they will act towards her the way she acted towards them. They might insist that she could hold it if she chose to. They might humiliate her by talking about her incontinence in front of others. They might not let her sit in their cars or visit their homes.

I usually think of the caregiver shadow as the Fascist. The caregiver shadow cannot get enough control: control of information, control of the schedule, control of medications, control of the environment, control of the money. Feedback is not allowed. Fascist regimes do not tolerate freedom of expression. Totalitarian caregiving can look good on the surface. It can even look like true devotion until one looks deeper and realizes that the stranglehold is choking out all the Mystery, all the Kairos, all the love.

One of my clients whose wife had isolated him from family and friends "for his own good" looked at me and asked me to pray that he would die soon. It was the only way he could get away from her. It reminded me of the famous scene in the movie *Whatever Happened to Baby Jane?* in which the psychotic Jane, played by Bette Davis, "takes care of" her invalid sister Blanche, played by Joan Crawford. After being served a lunch of stewed rat, Blanche complains, "Oh, Jane. You wouldn't treat me this way if I wasn't in a wheelchair." To which Baby Jane/Bette replies without hesitation, "But ya are in a wheelchair, Blanche. Ya are!"

Stressors

Various authors, such as Barbara Brown, a neurophysiologist who did pioneering work on stress and the brain and Hans Selye, a noted endocrinologist who first identified unhealthy stress as a factor underlying many diseases, draw a distinction between *healthy* and *unhealthy* stress or *distress*. Healthy stress is normal and necessary. For example, when we exercise we put stress on our bones, which increases their density and strength. Stress that imposes too great a burden over too long a time, however, can result in injury or permanent damage. (Brown 1984, 25-37)

Healthy stress and distress are the endpoints of a continuum. Distress is the *red zone*. Each individual will experience stress and distress differently depending on his or her unique circumstances. All individuals in a caregiving situation bring their particular stress/distress configuration to the mix. There are certain stressors that everyone, both sick and well, will likely experience in their encounter with illness and dying: boredom, smells, fatigue, burnout and the inevitable question Why Me?

I've never been in a sickroom where there wasn't some form of drama enacted at some time or another, from angry outbursts to serious confrontations. In almost every case, the people involved were stressed and distressed and behaving in ways very unlike their normal selves. This would not be a problem if we lived in a culture that held harmless anything said and done during times like this. But we do not. I've seen families split apart by words and actions that, except for the rawness of everyone's nerves, could have been seen as merely irritating instead of devastating.

The stressors I've identified are ones that I find personally challenging. Every person is different. I encourage the reader to identify his or her particular stressors. It is up to each of us to figure out our limits and get help designing appropriate supports. I really want to be there for the people I love. I don't want anything to get in the way. However, being human, I have my limits. Caregiving challenges me to respect my limits even if sometimes I have to go past those limits, knowing I'll pick up the tab later.

Boredom

The boredom of caregiving can drive you crazy. Over the years I've tried various ways to occupy myself so that I can stay present and not drive anyone too crazy. But illness can be boring not just for the caregiver but for the person in the bed as well. Acknowledging that both are bored can result in some rather creative ways of managing this particular stress. I've learned that being bored is not the worst thing that ever happened to me. Slowing down enables me to be more available in the present moment. It has enabled me to learn crafts like knitting and spinning. But the real gift of mutually acknowledging the boredom has been passing the time engaged in one of the oldest human activities, telling stories. I am always curious about the other person. Where have they lived? What adventures have they had? Tell me about your life before this all happened to you. Favorite movies? Authors? Pets? Ethnic background? Food can be a great topic depending on the person's condition. And, of course, relationships! Talking about former loves can while away an afternoon.

The Oxford Universal Dictionary tells us boredom means "to weary by tedious conversation or by failure to interest." We live in a culture where boredom is Public Enemy Number One. We're used to fast-paced dialogue in movies and on television. Advertising agencies spend millions of dollars designing ads that spark and hold our interest. Our drugs of choice are caffeine and adrenaline. We are the culture that invented the term multitask. What happens when a caffeinated multitasker visits a sickroom or sits for hours in a hospital waiting room? What happens when a caffeinated multitasker is discovered to have cancer or heart disease?

Most illnesses are chronic with acute episodes. There are exceptions such as certain kinds of cancer, but even these are becoming chronic as new treatments are devised. One comment I hear often from individuals recounting their first eight to twelve hours spent waiting in an emergency room is "it's not like on ER," referring to the fast-paced television show centered on the dramas of a Chicago emergency room. Or someone will say "can't we fast forward through this part?" Will the baby boomers invent a TV show called *The Waiting Room* or a reality show called *Living with a Chronic Diabetic*? It would be more fact-based. It would be like watching wallpaper peel. No drama, just daily life.

Here are some of my tried and true ways to cope with boredom. First, it's important to admit that one is bored. I always have various and sundry "things to do" like knitting or crossword puzzles. If I know that I am headed for a long wait (and I assume it will be a long wait), I always try to take a long walk or perform some other kind of strenuous exercise before I arrive. I try to remember that I'm not the only one who is bored. If I'm with other people we can devise distractions. Magazines like *Vanity Fair* and *People* are fun. Gossiping about friends can be enjoyable. Getting something to drink and sitting outside for a little while provides a break. If I'm alone and can't leave it gets more interesting in a perverse kind of way. Am I going to implode or explode? This is where I have to take myself in hand and remember why I'm there.

I am not there to be entertained. I am there to be of service. It's not about me. An adjunct to waiting room boredom is task boredom: doing the same thing day in and day out, the same round of appointments, the same litany of worries and complaints, the same stack of paperwork. Then there is the boredom of illness itself. After the drama of the tests and diagnosis and initial treatment, the grim reality begins: pills, special diets, side effects, pain and gnawing uncertainty about the future.

Caffeinated multitaskers don't handle the quotidian very well. We're caught up in our to-do lists and plans for the future. Performing required daily duties is an acquired taste. The mercy is that while the situation may be boring, the people never are.

Smells

Although I've entitled this section *Smells*, I mean to include all of the physical manifestations of illness that are enormously stressful to everyone involved. I'm talking about bodily fluids like sweat and drool and mucus and urine. I'm talking about bowel movements and gas and vomit. I'm talking about the smell of illness and the smell of medications.

Once most people lived on or near a farm, babies were born at home and indoor plumbing existed only in the mind of God. People lived with the associated unpleasant realities all the time. Now most of us work in offices. Bodily functions take place out of sight, births and deaths occur in special rooms and every effort is made to wipe out any unpleasant odors. This is the reason that most of us are completely unprepared for the reality of illness, our own or another's. On the one hand we are mature people, ready and willing to cope, and on the other we can be overwhelmed by the physical reality, which no amount of deodorant or cleaning fluid can eliminate.

I remember one man who kept repeating "this isn't my body." Nurses would assure him that it was his body and then privately advise a psychiatric consultation. But I had known him when he was a gorgeous, young athlete a lifetime away from the gaunt, hairless specter he had become with lesions and jutting bones.

It has taken time and effort to learn to tolerate the nastier aspects of sickness. What always works for me is to focus more on the person than on my discomfort. Protecting their pride is crucial. I think that the smells and other insults of illness are one of the major reasons that people don't visit the sick. All of our explanations aside, the realities of illness can be too grim, especially since the sick represent a probable future for us. This can be overwhelming for someone who prizes the illusion of his or her immortality.

It goes back to asking people about their fears, especially their fear of being "dirty." To be privy to such an intimate disclosure imposes a great responsibility. If I commit to protecting the person from their worst fear, I'd better be prepared to do the job myself if need be. Otherwise what was my promise worth?

Fatigue and Burnout

Much has been written about caregiver fatigue and burnout. A lot can be required of a caregiver on any given day. The list can be immense: grocery shopping, cooking, financial management, errands, housework, transportation, administering medications, giving shots, changing dressings, inserting feeding tubes, bathing, shaving, helping to the toilet, counseling, and the continuous duty of just watching over the care recipient.

This kind of workload sounds unbelievable until we remember the thousands of elderly couples where one spouse is taking care of the other or the middle-aged daughter taking care of her parents or in-laws. Imagine having the responsibility for all of these, day in and day out for years on end. Sometimes the reality is complicated by the fact that the elderly spouse has his or her own health issues or that the daughter has a job and family of her own to attend to.

This isn't burned out. This is burdened-out. Because burnout is a process and not a onetime event, perhaps a better term to use is *burning out*. Burning out is fueled by the accumulation of insults, the gap between expectations and reality, and clashes between individuals and corporate care delivery systems.

But the person needing care and the caregiver needn't be presented as complete opposites, the one totally helpless and dependent and the other burdened with the responsibility of care. This may be true in the final phase of illness or dementia, but I think it's important to note that throughout most of the illness process everyone, patient and caregivers included, has needs and responsibilities. We need to work towards reciprocal caring, collaboration and interdependence.

I have witnessed the heroic devotion of many spouses and children taking care of sick family members with long-term debilitating illnesses. I have also seen people crack under the strain. There is no safety net. Calling people heroic may be complimentary, but it seems inaccurate somehow. It isolates. People sometimes tell me that what I do is remarkable, so remarkable that they could not possibly do it. I tell them no, what I do is perfectly ordinary though hard; you can do it too. I don't want to be seen as special, a separate class. It makes something sentimental out of something that is heroic and horrific. These caregivers function as unpaid nurse's aides working round-the-clock shifts in homes across the nation. Burned out? How about used up? We're talking about hard labor with no time off for good behavior.

Burnout is one of those terms used so often it has almost become meaningless. It can be used as a diagnosis, explanation or justification. But what is it? I experience burnout as a complex mental and physical condition with three major components: feeling abused, feeling overextended, and feeling both totally responsible and completely powerless.

Feeling abused is extremely debilitating. Caregivers are often drafted into service by the needs of a loved one. Most have jobs outside the home. Balancing the needs of a cranky sick person, an inflexible medical system, and fears about the future while attempting to lead your own life can leave a person feeling trapped, unappreciated, unheard and disrespected.

Feeling physically, emotionally and financially over-extended day in and day out with no end in sight can be an enormous strain. There's not enough time, not enough money, not enough energy. All of this can result in not having enough patience or having difficulty processing new information and solving problems. Overexposed is a variation of overextended. Like overexposed film, the caregiver gets fuzzy around the edges. Events tend to blur.

Feeling paradoxically totally responsible and complete powerless is a frequent symptom of burnout. The caregiver can feel that the whole job is on his or her shoulders. Perhaps it is. But the course of the illness, the medical system, finances, family and friends are beyond the caregiver's control. In an effort to cope with such contradictory realities, the caregiver may take refuge at either end of the continuum, either attempting to control everyone and everything or giving up on the possibility to affect situation in any way.

The feeling of being in control of our lives is crucial to our sense of well-being. Little children go through an endearing phase where everything is *mine*: my mommy, my daddy, my puppy. Few of us outgrow this phase completely. Most of us get socialized into sharing. We learn to mimic the behavior of adults. At times I wonder how genuine our sharing really is. How many of us never outgrew this phase, but learned to mimic sharing behavior in order to please our parents and teachers? In the presence of sickness, how many of us regress to our childish selves? How many of us can depend on our learned sharing behavior? The person in need of care has a vital interest in the answers to these questions.

Why Me?

The question *Why Me?* is one that we all ask at some point or another in our lives. It can haunt both the person who is sick and the people responsible for caregiving. I'm sure other caregivers will agree that this question surfaces from time to time, especially when the fatigue is bone deep and the sense of being trapped is overwhelming. Why me? Why do I have to be here? This can lead to a cataract of questions. Am I the only one who cares? Why aren't others here carrying their share of the work? Why do they get to go on trips? Am I right? Are they? Am I being a martyr? Masochistic? Am I using this person's situation to avoid living my own life? Am I the only one who sees how at risk this person is in this hospice or alone here in his home? Am I just a control freak? Am I scared for no reason? When will I ever get enough sleep? Will I ever not be tired?

Service providers choose their profession. Most caregivers get drafted. Patients are drafted into illness when tests show a lump or a blockage or a failing vital organ. Caregivers are drafted when a loved one gets a diagnosis or a neighbor collapses in the hallway or an acquaintance from church gets hospitalized and has no one close by who can help.

Being a caregiver is like being a private in a large army. While some enlist as caregivers out of the goodness of their hearts, most people suddenly find themselves in this role. They awake to find themselves in basic training, receiving orders from medical personnel and insurance companies. Sickrooms are the front lines for most care, far removed from the orderly world inhabited by service providers who prescribe and schedule and issue to-do lists. This is a major component of the suffering surrounding illness. Your life is not your own. This was not a choice.

As a caregiver I have at times felt kidnapped. The British Navy once employed a tactic called impressment. If a ship didn't have a full complement of sailors, officers would go through a town and kidnap men who looked reasonably strong. Perhaps they were passed out drunk or they got knocked on the head. These men would wake up on a ship already miles out to sea with no choice but to make the best of it. One can only imagine their feelings when they awoke. How does one make the best of it? No doubt they asked *Why me?*

Opportunities for Repair

Many of us can remember Rosemary Clooney conjuring the image of an old man in a crumbling house seeing "an angel peekin' through a broken windowpane" in the song *This Ole House*.

> This ole house is a-gettin' shaky
> This ole house is a-gettin' old
> This ole house lets in the rain
> This ole house lets in the cold
>
> This ole house is afraid of thunder
> This ole house is afraid of storms
> This ole house just groans and trembles
> When the night wind flings its arms
>
> This ole house is gettin' feeble
> This old house is needin' paint
> Just like him it's tuckered out
> But he's a-gettin' ready to meet the saints

A decrepit old house and a dying old man: it's a pretty grim picture. In other verses the song mentions a wife and children, laughter and comfort. I wonder what happened to them. Did the old man simply outlive everyone he knew? Did his children leave and never come back? Did he drive them away? His house is collapsing around him. It no longer matters. He is dying. The time for doing repairs has run out.

When I searched the web for the words to this song I mistakenly entered "This Old House." In response I got all sorts of websites related to the TV program *This Old House,* the godfather of TV home improvement shows. What a contrast. No unchecked decrepitude for these folks! Nor are we likely to see them purchasing a new home in a manicured subdivision, choosing from an array of pre-form models promising a classy turnkey living. Instead they encourage us to explore old houses and find the bones. Trades people in jeans and wearing tool belts extol the adventures that can lie behind our outdated wallpaper and under our bathroom tile.

I imagine a crew of these tool-belted warriors showing up at This *Ole* House with ladders, shingles and paint. I think this attitude towards rehabilitating old structures represents a welcome change in our society: choosing to adapt decades-old structures to contemporary needs and modern technology, committing time and money to make the changes, living with the mess of the work-in-progress, and being open to learning new skills.

Instead of traveling to the edge of town and building new, we are learning how to work with structures inherited from previous generations. When I was growing up, people redecorated or made surface modifications. Today they gut the place and renovate it. Homeowners carry the costs and endure the inconveniences, adapting old structures to modern tastes and contemporary needs. They might even do some of the work themselves.

Which brings me to my point. When death is in the house it can be crucial to shift the family model from "This *Ole* Family" to "This *Old* Family," from a model of family that exemplifies hopeless disintegration to one that is basically hopeful, acknowledging opportunities for repairs and modification. The same kind of choices apply in caregiving as apply in house renovation: choosing to adapt to contemporary needs and modern technology, committing time and money to make the changes, living with the mess of the work-in-progress, and being open to learning new skills.

According to a recent New York Times article, there are about twenty million baby boomers coping with the needs of aging or ailing parents. How many of them are trying to accomplish this care in family relationship structures that are outmoded or in desperate need of repair? Caring for aging, ailing parents is hard enough in *This Old Family house*. It can be a nightmare in *This Ole Family house*.

Fortunately there can be many opportunities for repair and enough time to make the changes *if a family starts early enough*. Different schools of therapy offer tools for making assessments and repairing fractured family relationships. For example: Family Systems Theory addresses problems of communication; Attachment Theory is concerned with relationship patterns laid down in early childhood; Intergenerational Family Therapy deals with unresolved issues passed from one generation to another; and research on the aging brain confronts problems such as decline in mental processing and depression.

Usually we think of psychotherapy as an exercise in looking at the past to explain the present and to provide remedies for current pain. Some may consider it a luxury and others a stigma. Illness and dying always bring pain and suffering. We can alleviate or prevent some of that pain and suffering by doing repairs and remodeling *This Old Family house.*

Medical science has expanded the amount of time between diagnosis and death for most illnesses. In my experience, focus on the family only occurs toward the end of life, with the emphasis on grief work. The healthcare delivery model is organized by and for service providers who provide their services in professional settings and almost never visit the home where the caregiving occurs. They seldom meet the family members whose interactions are such a critical factor in the environment.

What if we could work with families early in the illness process? What if we could bring in the family systems version of a general contractor to evaluate the ability of a family structure to withstand the stress events that are coming? What if this Family Systems Contractor could provide a status report with recommendations for repairs? What if the family committed time and resources to working on the most serious problems?

I know this can sound very pie-in-the-sky. Families struggling with all the complexities of caregiving might find it inconceivable to take on one more challenge. Yet I have seen the kind of difference this effort can make in alleviating a lot of stress for everyone involved. Caregiving can go on for years. Not doing these kinds of repairs is like taking care of someone in a house with broken windows and poor wiring. The job is hard enough. Why make it harder?

Can't and Won't

One of the most common examples of caregiver stress can be the contest of wills between the caregiver and the person receiving care. Sometimes it is simply a replay of a lifelong power struggle, the kind of nattering that married couples do. Sometimes it is an effort by the person receiving care to set a boundary, have some autonomy. Sometimes it is pure contrariness. If both people are relatively well and independent, there is little harm and maybe even some good in this contest. The more tired the caregiver, however, and the more dependent the person receiving care, such contests can escalate into serious confrontations and even abuse on both sides.

Many people tend to use the words *can't* and *won't* interchangeably although they have very different meanings. *Can't*, means *unable.* *Won't*, means *able but unwilling.* *Can't* is a fixed condition. *Won't* is a choice. Technically if someone can't do something, there is no contest of wills. Yet time and again I have seen people refuse to accept the fact that someone has lost the ability to do something: control bowels and urine, swallow solid food, remember names, tie shoes, button buttons, manage silverware.

I've seen family members yell at incapacitated loved ones, mock or refuse to help them, force food into their mouths, refuse to use diapers, all with the conviction that the person is simply refusing to cooperate. Sometimes caregivers take it as defiance or even as a personal attack. So much pain is caused by ignorance. In most cases these are well-meaning people acting out old patterns. Caregiving stressors exacerbate old wounds. The siege mentality of many caregivers makes it difficult to get new information across.

This is the kind of mental processing error that can be discovered early in the caregiving process. The caregiver can be aware that under stress he or she may see defiance and attack where there is actually incapacity. Every one has a breaking point at which they regress to primal instincts and primitive behaviors. Wouldn't it be wonderful to find that breaking point *before* it breaks and to do the necessary repairs before real damage is done?

Saying Thank You

The *Thank You Test* is a wonderful diagnostic tool. Does the client ever say Thank You? Does the caregiver ever express gratitude for this opportunity to show love-in-action or to practice altruism or to learn about illness, dying and death? Gratitude is much more than the etiquette of thank you notes, although these can be a wonderful gesture. Gratitude is more like a relationship lubricant: it keeps the elements of the community engine moving smoothly. The absence of gratitude might indicate a kind of tone-deafness to others' feelings, a lack of skill in expressing gratitude, a backlog of unresolved resentments, an exaggerated sense of entitlement, or an unwillingness to admit the need for or anger about needing care. Some people believe that paying for a service cancels the need for gratitude, whether that payment was in the past (I gave you life), the present (I'm paying you for service), or the future (I'm leaving you money in my will).

The absence of gratitude can contribute to anger and increased resentment as the workload increases. How can these issues be addressed? I usually tackle it head on by pointing out that I need to be thanked from time to time. I am not a piece of furniture or a robot. I need to know that I'm appreciated. It has to do with being recognized, being seen. I also periodically express my gratitude for the opportunity to be of service. I really want to be of service to people, particularly during the events of illness and dying. To do that I need people who are willing to let me into their lives at these times of crisis. I have a lot to give but there has to be someone to receive it. I appreciate when someone who is willing to let me exercise my gifts.

Confronting the issue of gratitude might reveal that there is none. The person being cared for might be so filled with rage and entitlement that there is no gratitude. The caregiver might be so tired and resentful at the burden that any sense of gift or opportunity has been leached from the situation. I've been there. I had one man living in my apartment for six weeks while we waited for a hospice bed to become available. I had a one-bedroom apartment and I gave him the bedroom. Not once did he say thank you. Not a gesture. Not a dime. Nothing. Mostly he complained. I was furious.

Appreciating and acknowledging the giver and the gift takes time and requires opening the boundaries of the self to include another person. The defensive stance needs to relax into receptivity. Gratitude makes us vulnerable for a time. Working with families might first require Gratitude Appreciation 101. If the situation is short term it might not matter. If it will be a siege, then I recommend working with a counselor or therapist to develop skills and resolve old resentments. Gratitude is basically about acknowledging the other. In his book *Gratefulness, the Heart of Prayer,* David Steindal-Rast quotes the proverb: "When you drink from a stream, remember the stream" (Steindal-Rast 2001, 3).

Saying I'm Sorry

I'm sorry is another great diagnostic. Even more than *thank you,* difficulties with saying *I'm sorry* are predictors of future trouble. To say *I'm sorry* is to admit that another person exists, that you are capable of doing harm, that you committed an offense, that you feel bad about your behavior. Saying I'm sorry means admitting these things and creating the space for a response.

People naturally prefer to forgive rather than to ask for forgiveness. It's a more powerful position. It can make us feel righteous. In a law-and-order culture that divides the world into victims and perpetrators, our sympathy is for the victim, the underdog. What can be really frustrating, however, is when everybody in a caregiving situation sees themselves as "more sinned against than sinning." A lot of people are getting hurt, but no one is admitting their complicity. Most people are oblivious to the harm they cause. Self-examination is often derided as navel-gazing or pathological self-attack. We consult professionals and self-help books to build self-esteem and a healthy self-image. A healthy self-image, however, encompasses both the light and the dark sides of our nature.

How do we deal with these blind spots? They can present serious problems resulting in all sorts of unchecked bad behavior. I remember one woman who looked me in the eye and said that in all her years she had never done anything wrong; she had never hurt anyone. Her demeanor was calm. Her expression was proud, almost smug. I then looked at her husband who suffered her neglect and daily verbal abuse about his incontinence. She saw herself as the victim of her husband's Parkinson's disease and was completely unconscious of any wrongs she had inflicted. Her husband told me privately that he just wanted to die so it would all be over. Her circle of friends and attending medical professionals reinforced her martyrdom. I was never able to move her toward any kind of self-examination. Her husband finally died. His ordeal was over.

There is such a thing as bad behavior. Humans do terrible things to each other. That is why we have laws against child and elder abuse. The problem is that these laws apply only after the crimes have been committed. So much pain could be prevented if individuals could understand that their behavior is causing pain and enter into a process of self-examination. Was it a mistake? A misunderstanding? Did they mean to cause harm?

How can we foster family cultures that support self-questioning and the establishment of standards of acceptable behavior? Most families have a backlog of offenses to address. For a family to move beyond past behavioral patterns into a coherent present, it somehow needs to get past accusations and recriminations to the actual painful events that caused them. We are all both sinned against and sinners. We are all flawed beings. Accepting this reality makes repair work possible.

I have been at many deathbeds and never once have I heard a person pronounce his or her forgiveness of others. Mostly I hear defenseless, tearful, tentative hopes for forgiveness. Unfortunately, the person they are reaching out to usually isn't there to hear.

How much unresolved grief is fueled by lack of forgiveness and lack of forgiving?

Saying Good-Bye

Many books on dying and death focus on the need to say and the negative consequences of not saying *good-bye*. Survivors often express deep regret that they did not say good-bye. Personally this has always seemed a non-issue. I have often wondered what the fuss is about. I just chalk it up to my not being a very sentimental type. I get to say so many good-byes with a small g that the Final Good-Bye is often an anti-climax.

What is the significance of *good-bye*? We say it when we leave a person or a place. We say it to acknowledge that someone is leaving us. Seems simple. Then why is it such a source of pain and real trauma? What if you've never really said *Hello* to begin with? What if you've never experienced the person to whom you're saying good-bye as a separate and distinct entity? Perhaps you took the person for granted. Suddenly they are thrust into the foreground of your life. Soon they will be gone. Perhaps they already are. Saying good-bye can be an emotional tsunami.

It's been said that you can pick your friends but you can't pick your family. In the movie of our lives, we are the stars. We may or may not have a co-star. Friends and colleagues play supporting roles. Family members are more likely to be seen as extras. Very seldom do we say hello to family members. When the time comes to say good-bye to them, all sorts of emotional hell can break loose. We may deny that there is any departure on the horizon. We may be angry at the disruption to our story. If we've never said hello, saying good-bye can shock our orderly world.

The more I think about it, saying *hello* is the first step in learning to say *thank you*, *I'm sorry*, and *good-bye*. To say *hello* is to acknowledge another person. How wonderful and terrible to acknowledge that there is someone in the universe besides me. What would it be like for families to discover each other before the ultimate good-bye? How can we foster this kind of discovery, these *hellos*?

Leaving a Legacy

Life is about matter. In the process of dying we shed layers of matter and we discover what matters. The layers of matter become the stuff of our estate. What matters to us becomes our legacy. Sometimes the dying process is described as the caterpillar on its way to becoming a butterfly. I think the empty husk is the stuff in our estate. The butterfly is our legacy. Unfortunately some butterflies are forever trapped in their cocoons. Some emerge but are too mangled to fly.

Another way to describe our legacy is to ask ourselves what we have wrought in our personal world. How has our living affected those we leave behind? What is our emotional legacy? What is our ethical legacy? Will the way we conducted ourselves and our affairs during the final years of our lives leave our loved ones light and free or will it leave them mired in guilt and divisiveness? Is our legacy one of order and thoughtfulness or will people be struggling to sort out our affairs and ascertain our wishes. Did we take responsibility for our messes and work to clean them up or did our final years become seedbeds for more confusion, guilt, jealousy and resentment?

Often people who are sick and approaching death develop what I call a kind of pathological narcissism. Everything is about their needs, their wishes and their worldview. Some of this is completely understandable. All of us regress when we are sick. Pain, weakness and fear activate the more primitive layers of the self. The organism's desire to live can overwhelm more lofty concerns. The shadow side of the self can create an unholy alliance with the drive to live at all costs.

The normal, life-affirming narcissism of an infant can become lethal in an adult. The time and resources of family and friends can be cannibalized without a thought. Life wants to live. This kind of pathological narcissism can drive everyone into a fight for survival. The legacy can be more like a mad competition for resources than the celebration of a harvest.

What would our legacy be if we were to die today? How do we want to leave this world? What do we want to leave this world? If we have the courage, we can describe what we want our legacy to be. Constructing our autobiographies can help us to understand how illness affects us, to understand the lineaments of our shadow selves and the infant needs that can morph into hungry ghosts for whom there is never enough. While we are well and strong we can contemplate these realities. We can communicate our hopes for our legacy and work with those who love us to make it happen.

Apprenticeships

An apprentice is someone committed to learning a skill from a master practitioner. In times past a family would pay a master craftsperson to train their child in a particular trade. The apprentice did all the grunt work around the shop. It wasn't a glamorous position, but it afforded the opportunity to learn all aspects of a trade and the kind of training one can't get in books.

I have been asked many times if I am interested in teaching a class about death and caregiving. I would much prefer to work with individuals to set up a kind of apprenticeship within an organized support structure. Caregiving is a craft. As in all crafts, an apprentice acquires skills with practice; he or she learns the vocabulary and philosophy and discovers wonderful opportunities for creativity. It is a tragedy that many caregivers get trapped in the drudgery and never get to the good part. And there is a good part! It might be the sense of a job well done. It might be a moment of laughter or tears. It might be the chance to alleviate pain. It might be witnessing a reconciliation. It might be a glimpse of love in action. It might be the sense that one is the right person in the right place at the right time.

When faced with the unknown, we seek information from others in conversations, support groups and books. Information is almost a sacrament in our culture. But information is not enough. A person can starve to death reading a cookbook. Caregiving, like cooking, requires skill and knowledge gained from experience, from *participation*. We learn by doing. Information gleaned from outside sources may be helpful, but it doesn't involve the senses. Participating in an event taps all the senses. There is a difference between a family dining out at a restaurant and the whole family creating a holiday meal at home.

Human events take place in real time. We can't fast forward to skip the bad or boring parts. Nor can we skip to the end to stop the suspense. We must deal with real life events as they occur. There are no scripts. We must surrender to the demands of the events. When we bake a cake, we surrender to the demands of the recipe. Specific ingredients in fixed amounts must be combined in a certain way and cooked a certain amount of time at a fixed temperature. We may dirty dishes and countertops in the process, but gradually the kitchen fills with the wonderful odors of baking.

My advice to prospective caregivers is to apprentice to someone who is chronically ill and then to someone who is dying. Make a contract. Agree to perform certain tasks. Set a time limit. Reach an understanding with the person about how much of their process they are willing to share. Keep a journal of your experiences. Find someone else with whom to process your experiences.

As an apprentice you commit to doing real work for this person such as helping with transportation, laundry and shopping and providing respite for other caregivers. You earn your right to be at intimate events by sharing in the grunt work. Some people, inspired by recent writings and programs about death and dying, want to *sit* with the dying. The reality is that there is precious little sitting happening, especially at a home death. Taking care of someone who is very ill is like taking care of a baby, except this baby weighs a lot and is often very verbal.

The times for sitting usually occur late at night, during the last few days of a person's life, and after the person dies. Till then, there are a thousand and one things to do, especially laundry. Often the dying person doesn't mind if you fold laundry in their room. Companioning can take many forms.

In the course of providing needed services as an apprentice, you can soak up the atmosphere and get a felt sense of the timing of caregiving. You also get first hand experience and the one luxury of being a grunt: no responsibility.

One can obtain such experience by volunteering with a local hospice program. I think it is wiser to start by working with a stranger. It is easier to see the transference and projections. There is less pressure and more space to think about the realities of illness, dying and death. When we start our caregiving with a loved one, the situation is automatically more loaded. We are less objective. Our pain and fear can make it hard to center and to learn.

Taking Charge of the Inevitable

Individuals do not approach sickness and dying as blank slates. They have complex autobiographies and relationship histories. Each of us carries the history of the wounds inflicted by the "slings and arrows of outrageous fortune," broken bones badly set, which forever ache and might break again under too much stress.

Sickness and dying can function like x-rays, exposing old injuries in everyone involved. What a nightmare. What an opportunity. Providing care can be a means of healing both the present and the past. If we remedy present ills with skill and compassion, we just might give everyone involved a new start in life. The stressful indignities of illness—difficulty eating, using the toilet, getting dressed, sleeping, taking medications, dealing with side effects, managing pain—also offer opportunities for repair.

Given that most of us will care for loved ones and ultimately need caregiving ourselves, often overlapping, it makes sense to be proactive. Aging comes on slowly. Most illnesses start small. There is time at the beginning of the process to reflect and to plan. Our fast-paced, crowded lives send us careening from one situation to another. Everything is urgent. Sometimes sudden events require urgent attention. But sudden events often aren't truly sudden at all. In retrospect we see that the signs were right there in front of us all along: mom's increasing confusion, dad's growing frailty, a friend's deepening pallor and fatigue. The urgent event—mom getting lost in the shopping mall, dad falling, our friend's collapse—crashes through our walls of distraction to grab out attention.

Disability, illness, dying and death are excluded from our media, workplace and conversations. Then suddenly a storm breaks with a heart attack, tumor or stroke. But the clouds had been gathering for years. It was only a matter of time. The sheer numbers of aging and ailing baby boomers combined with shrinking social services, uncertain retirement funds and complex medical management at home portend that we will have to rely on our communities of families, friends and neighbors for care in the future. Many of us will end up needing more care than we can pay for. We might well be dependent on "the kindness of strangers." *This Old Family* house might have to be remodeled so it can stand up to these harsh realities. Doesn't it make good sense to remodel the house before the storm breaks?

At different times with various clients I have attended meetings with accountants, estate planners, attorneys, psychologists, doctors and priests. In almost every instance these meetings helped to reduce confusion and contribute to an increased sense of peace. However, the problem was that the meetings usually took place late in the game. The general sense among the participants was that much more could have been accomplished if the work had begun sooner. The goal was to put out immediate fires: writing a will; scrambling for caregiving resources; resolving the ambiguities of an unexamined life. There was often no coordination among the professionals providing advice. Information was passed from person to person with outcomes similar to those in the game of Telephone played at children's parties.

I believe that what is needed is a program designed for families or groups of friends who want to be proactive about the inevitable. The goal of this program would be to provide a holistic approach to the illness and dying process, interweaving a wide array of end-of-life issues with the intention of gathering all the various threads of a life together so that, like fabric coming off of a loom, the life maintains its integrity to its completion.

Participants in the program, recognizing that illness and death are inevitable and making use of available information, will organize their affairs to prevent as much trauma as possible to their loved ones, both before and after they die. Participants could include individuals who have been made aware of their mortality by a recently diagnosed potentially terminal illness; those who have just lost a loved one; those trying to be proactive about their own eventual aging process; families caring for a member diagnosed with a serious illness or trying to come to terms with the reality of aging parents; long-standing intimates committed to designing ways to care for each other in the face of illness and aging in the absence of blood relations.

The program would make use of an interdisciplinary team of providers experienced in end-of-life issues including accountants, estate planners, tax experts, medical advisors, psychologists, social workers, clergy and funeral planners. Given that the individuals coming to them for assistance in organizing their affairs are part of a community, these providers would commit to developing strategies that attend to the needs of both the individuals and their communities. They would be aware that these strategies ensure the clients' rights to privacy while at the same time encourage full communication with and among participants, recognizing that information needs to be imparted with careful attention to content, timing, impact and differing information processing styles.

Program participants would concentrate on dealing with all aspects of a person's needs—medical, legal, personal, spiritual, business, relationships, leaving a legacy—with the purpose of developing communication skills, clarifying values, determining rights and responsibilities, and resolving conflicts. Participants would ascertain the existence and location of all important business, legal and medical documents; evaluate family relationship strengths, stressors and unresolved tensions; explore the family's history of dealing with illness, caregiving, death and grief; determine the current health status and care needs of family members; evaluate the distribution of current caregiving workloads and the nature of the caregiving environment; anticipate the probable course of illness and future needs for care; estimate financial needs and recommend strategies for dealing with projected shortfalls; and identify current and potential problem areas, recommending strategies for prevention or repair.

A participant group would have a central team coordinator who would be the *go-to* person for coordinating needs-assessments, meetings with consultants, and providing on-going support for implementation of the initial plan. Given the likelihood that participants would already be working with their own attorneys, accountants, medical specialists, etc., the team coordinator, with the permission of the participants, would communicate with each of these consultants about the goals of the program team-building effort. The team would provide initial evaluation and long-term assistance to a family or group of caregivers on an as-needed basis with the emphasis on accurate information, clear communication and problem solving. The goal would be to support and balance the needs of everyone in the Caregiving Zone as the situation unfolded.

I get very excited about the prospect of such teams. Just think how much learning could happen with this kind of resource. Imagine how much pain could be prevented. Potentially lethal family landmines, such as long-held secrets or old guilt, could be avoided or harmlessly exploded. Individuals could be alerted to the long-term consequences of a badly written trust or inequities in a bequest. Family members and long-standing intimates could make informed decisions about allocating resources over time. There could be opportunity for addressing and resolving sibling issues, rifts with friends, and spiritual dilemmas. Much of the confusion, blame and guilt that create a lot of the toxicity in grief could be eliminated.

This experience need not be dire or gloomy. Families might enjoy discovering their history through genealogy and genograms. Individuals might increase their sense of fulfillment as they bring to light buried dreams and perhaps commit to making them real. Formerly unarticulated spiritual longings and questions could be explored. Writing an autobiography or collection of family stories can be a gift to the self as well as future generations. Optimally, the program would be an ongoing source of informed support as other members of the group face illness, dying and death. The group would be able to call upon and make use of its combined experience and skills. As the group becomes more and more adept at coping with end-of-life issues, perhaps the overall level of fear among its members would diminish. The realities of illness and death are never easy, but they can be made less difficult.

Making Stone Soup

Often when people ask me to describe my preferred end-stage care scenario, I tell them the story of *Stone Soup*. Most people think of it as a children's story, but it is more of a folk tale. There are many versions of this story. In Scandanavia and northern European countries it's called Nail Soup. The Portuguese version locates the story in Almeirim, Portugal where many restaurants still serve stone soup (sopa de pedra). In Eastern Europe the story is called Axe Soup. The newcomers to the village in the story change identities in the various versions. In some stories it's a troop of soldiers, in others a wandering priest, peddler or tramp. Sometimes the participants are experiencing a famine, sometimes a war. In every case, they want nothing to do with a stranger whom they see as having designs on their food, which they have taken the precaution of hiding. The strangers' requests for food and shelter are met with claims of poverty.

Here's the story.

Three soldiers were walking down a road in a strange country on their way home from a war. They were tired and hadn't eaten for days.

"How I would like a good dinner tonight!" said the first. "And a bed to sleep in!" added the second. "But that's impossible," complained the third.

Ahead of them, they saw the lights of a village. "Maybe we'll find a bite to eat and a bed to sleep in," they thought.

The village peasants, fearing strangers and hearing that three soldiers were coming their way, talked among themselves. "Soldiers are always hungry, and we have so little for ourselves," they said. They hurriedly hid their food. They put barley in haylofts, kept carrots under quilts, and poured milk down wells. They hid everything and waited.

The soldiers stopped at the first house.

"Good evening to you," they said. "Could you spare a bit of food for three hungry soldiers?"

"We have no food for ourselves. We had a poor harvest," said the man at the door.

The soldiers went to the next house. "Could you spare a bit of food?" they asked. "And do you have a corner where we could sleep for the night?"

"Oh, no," the man said. "We gave all we could spare to the soldiers who came before you and our beds are full."

At each house, the response was the same. No one had food or a place for the soldiers to stay. The villagers all had good reasons for their inhospitality: they had given their food to the sick and to needy children. They sighed and tried to look hungry.

After conversing with each other one of the soldiers called out, "Good people! We are three hungry soldiers in a strange land. We have asked you for food and you have none. Well, we will have to make stone soup."

The peasants were confused and stared at the soldiers in disbelief as they asked for a big iron pot, water to fill it, fire to heat it, and three smooth round stones, which they dropped into the pot.

"Every soup needs seasonings," the first soldier said. Some children ran to fetch them salt and pepper.

"Stone soup is good, but carrots make it so much better," the second soldier noted. "I think I have a carrot or two!" said one woman, scurrying to her house.

"A really good stone soup should have cabbage. What a shame we don't have any!" said the third soldier. "I can probably find some cabbage," said another woman.

"If only we had a bit of beef and some potatoes, then this soup would be fit for a rich man's table," said the first soldier. The peasants talked it over. A rich man's soup! And all from a few stones! It seemed like magic! They ran to fetch what they had hidden in their cellars.

The soldiers said, "If we had a bit of barley and some milk, this soup would be fit for a king!" Barley and milk were provided.

"The soup is ready," said the cooks, "and all will taste it, but first we need to set the tables." Tables and torches were set up in the square and all sat down to eat. Some of the peasants said, "Such a great soup would be better with bread and cider," so they brought forth these last two items. Never had there been such a feast in the village. Never had the peasants tasted such delicious soup. And all made from stones! They ate, drank and danced well into the night.

The soldiers asked again if there was a humble loft where they might sleep for the night. "Oh, no!" said the townsfolk. "You must have the best beds in the village!" One soldier spent the night in the priest's house, one in the baker's house, and one in the mayor's house.

In the morning, the villagers gathered to say goodbye and thank the strangers. "We shall never go hungry now that you have taught us how to make soup from stones!"

Illness and death are always unfamiliar, unwelcome and disturbing when they stop to visit us personally. The reaction of friends and family of those afflicted is often the same: circle the wagons, plead poverty of time and money, hope it goes away. What making stone soup illustrates to me is that quite a feast can be made if everybody shares a little. Some cynics may remark on how easily the villagers were duped into sharing and how naïve they were to believe in soup made with stones. But I see it a different way. The peasants were understandably afraid of losing their supplies to strange soldiers entering their town. Suspicion of soldiers or any stranger is a necessary precaution. These soldiers, however, offer them a way out of their fear and suspicion and a way into a celebration. And they go for it.

Living in the Caregiving Zone can be like being in a village shut tight against intruders, or it can be a feast where everyone contributes what they can. Communitas is what happens when, for a time, people are coaxed out from behind their barricades by the promise of good food made from rock-hard realities.

References

Becker, Ernest. *The Denial of Death*. New York: Free Press Paperbacks, Simon & Schuster, 1973.

Bernard RN, Jan S. & Schneider RN, Miriam. *The True Work of Dying*. New York: Avon Books, 1996.

Blau MD, Sheldon & Shimberg, Elaine. *How to Get Out of the Hospital Alive: A Guide to Patient Power*. New York: MacMillian, 1997.

Boerstler, Richard W. & Kornfeld, Hulen S. *Life to Death*. Vermont: Healing Arts Press, 1995.

Bolen M.D., Jean Shinoda. *Close to the Bone*. New York: Simon and Schuster, 1996.

Bowen MD, Murray. *Family Therapy in Clinical Practice*. Northvale, New Jersey: Jason Aronson, 2002.

Bowlby, John. *Attachment and Loss: Vol. 1. Attachment*. New York: Basic Books, 1969, 1982.

————. *Attachment and Loss: Vol. 2. Separation: Anxiety and Anger*. New York: Basic Books, 1973.

————. *Attachment and Loss: Vol. 3. Loss: Sadness and Depression*. New York: Basic Books, 1980.

Brown, Barbara. *Between Health and Illness*. Boston: Houghton Mifflin Company, 1984.

Bruyere, Rosalyn. *Wheels of Light*. New York: Simon and Schuster, 1989.

Buber, Martin. *I and Thou*. Translated by Ronald Gregor Smith. New York: Charles Scribner's Sons, 1958.

Byock MD, Ira. *Dying Well.* New York: Riverhead Books, 1997.

Callanan, Maggie & Kelly, Patricia. *Final Gifts.* New York: Bantam Books, 1993.

Capossela, Cappy, and Sheila Warnock. *Share the Care.* New York: Simon & Schuster, 1995.

Carter, Rosalynn. *Helping Someone with Mental Illness.* New York: Three Rivers Press, 1998.

———. *Helping Yourself Help Others.* New York: Three Rivers Press, 1995.

Devine CM, Richard J. *Good Care, Painful Choices.* Mahwah, NJ: Paulist Press, 1996.

Donchin, Anne. "Autonomy, Interdependence, and Assisted Suicide." *Bioethics* 14, no. 3 (2000): 187-204.

Donovan, Jean. *The Mystery of Death.* Mahwey, NJ: Paulist Press, 2003.

Elison EdD., Jennifer & McGonigle Ph.D., Chris. *Liberating Losses.* Cambridge, MA: Perseus Publishing, 2003.

Emmons, Robert A., and Joanna Hill. *Words of Gratitude for Mind, Body, and Soul.* West Conshohocken, PA: Templeton Foundation Press, 2001.

Felder PhD, Leonard. *When a Loved One is Ill.* New York: NAL Books, 1990.

Furman MSN RN, Joan, and David McNabb. *The Dying Time.* New York: Bell Tower, 1997.

Golden RN, Susan. *Nursing a Loved One at Home.* Philadelphia, PA: Running Press, 1988.

Guggenbuhl-Craig, Adolf. *Power in the Helping Professions.* Translated by Myron Grubitz. Woodstock, Conn.: Spring Publications, 1971.

Guroian, Vigen. *Life's Living Toward Dying.* Grand Rapids, Michigan: Eerdmans Publishing, 1996.

Harrold MD, Joan, and Joanne Lynn MD. *A Good Dying.* New York: The Haworth Press, 1998.

Hennezel, Marie de. *Intimate Death, How the Dying Teach Us How to Live*. New York: Vintage Books, 1998.

Hesse, Erik, and Mary Main. "Disorganized Infant, Child, and Adult Attachment: Collapse in Behavioral and Attentional Strategies." *Journal of the American Psychoanalytic Association* (New York) 48, no. 4 (2000): 1097-127.

Humphry, Derek. *Final Exit*. New York: Dell Publishing, 1991.

Jordan, Michael. *Ceremonies for Life*. London: Collins & Brown Limited, 2001.

Jung, C. G. *Two Essays on Analytical Psychology*. 1943; 1945. Translated by R. F. C. Hull. Cleveland, OH: The World Publishing Company, 1953.

Karel, M., S. Ogland-Hand, and M. Gatz. *Assessing and Treating Late Life Depression*. New York: Basic Books, 2002.

Kaufman, Sharon R. *And a Time to Die*. New York: Scribner, 2005.

Klein, Allen. *The Courage to Laugh*. New York: Penguin Putnam, 1998.

Knight, Bob. *Psychotherapy with Older Adults*. Beverly Hills, CA: Sage Publications, Inc., 1986.

Kubler-Ross, Elizabeth. *On Death and Dying*. New York: Macmillan Publishing Company, 1969.

Lerner, Michael. *The Left Hand of God*. San Francisco, CA: HarperCollins, 2006.

Lynn MD, Joanne, and Joan Harrold MD. *Handbook for Mortals*. New York: Oxford University Press, 1999.

Main, Mary. "Epilogue, Attachment Theory: Eighteen Points." In *Handbook of Attachment Theory, Research, and Clinical Applications*, edited by Jude Cassidy and Phillip R. Shaver, 845-87. New York: The Guilford Press, 1999.

———. "The Organized Categories of Infant, Child, and Adult Attachment: Flexible Vs. Inflexible Attention Under Attachment-Related Stress." *Jour-*

nal of the American Psychoanalytic Association (New York) 48, no. 4 (2000): 1055-96.

Martin, Sheila. *Saying Goodbye With Love*. New York: Crossroad Publishing Company, 1996.

McGoldrick, Monica. *The Legacy of Unresolved Loss (Video)*. New Jersey: The Multicultural Family Institute, 1991.

Meltzer, David, ed. *Death: An Anthology of Ancient Texts, Songs, Prayers, and Stories*. San Francisco, CA: North Point Press, 1984.

Morris, Virginia. *Talking About Death Won't Kill You*. New York, NY: Workman Publishing, 2001.

Nuland, Sherwin B. *How We Die*. New York: Alfred A. Knopf, 1994.

Parker, Susan. *Tumbling After*. New York: Crown Publishers, 2002.

Polster, Erving. *Every Person's Life is Worth A Novel*. W.W. Norton & Company, 1987.

Quill, Timothy E. *Midwife Through the Dying Process*. Maryland: Johns Hopkins University Press, 1996.

Radin, Lisa and Gary, eds. *What If It's Not Alzheimers?* New York, NY: Prometheus Books, 2003.

Rahner SJ, Karl. *Encounters with Silence*. Translated by James M. Demske SJ. South Bend, Indiana: St. Augustine's Press, 1999.

Register, Cheri. *The Chronic Illness Experience*. Hazelden, Minnesota, 1987.

Rinpoche, Sogyal. *The Tibetan Book of Living and Dying*. New York: Harper Collins, 1993.

Roach CSM, M. Simone, ed. *Caring from the Heart: The Convergence of Caring and Spirituality*. Mahwah, NJ: Paulist Press, 1997.

Sardello, Robert. *Facing the World with Soul*. Hudson, NY: Lindisfarne Press, 1992.

Selye, Hans. *The Stress of Life*. New York: McGraw-Hill, 1956.

Siegel, Daniel J. *The Developing Mind*. New York: The Guilford Press, 1999.

Steindl-Rast, Br. David, and Henri J. M. Nouwen. *Gratefulness The Heart of Prayer*. Ramsey, NJ: Paulist Press, 1984.

Steinfels, Peter & Veatch, Robert. *Death Inside Out*. New York: Harper & Row, Publishers, 1974.

SteinhoffSmith, Roy Herndon. *The Mutuality of Care*. Missouri: Chalice Press, 1999.

Stern, MD, Daniel N. *The Present Moment in Psychotherapy and Everyday Life*. New York: W. W. Norton, 2004.

Tannen PhD, Deborah. *You Just Don't Understand*. New York: Ballantine Books, 1990.

Turner, Victor. *From Ritual to Theatre*. New York: PAJ Publications, 1982.

———. *The Ritual Process*. Ithaca, New York: Cornell University Press, 1969.

Volicer MD PhD, Ladislav and Hurley RN, Ann. *Hospice Care for Patients with Advanced Progressive Dementia*. New York: Springer Publications, 1998.

Volk, Tyler. *What is Death?* New York: John Wiley & Sons, 2002.

Walsh, Froma and Monica McGoldrick. *Living Beyond Loss*. New York: W. W. Norton, 2004.

Webb, Marilyn. *The Good Death*. New York: Bantam Books, 1999.

Weenolsen PhD, Patricia. *Art of Dying*. New York: St. Martin's Press, 1996.

Internet Resources

Rosalynn Carter Institute for Caregiving. http://rci.gsw.edu.

Caregiver.Com. www.caregiver.com.

Family Caregiver Alliance. www.caregiver.org.

Compassion & Choices. www.compassionandchoices.og.

Growth House. www.growthhouse.org.

The Good Death Institute. www.tgdi.org

The Hastings Center. www.thehastingscenter.prg.

WebMD. www.webmd.com.

Medline Plus. www.medlineplus.gov.

978-0-595-40649-4
0-595-40649-1